From Tired to Inspired

Dr. Deonne Johnson

A Soulful Guide to Reclaim Your
Energy, Joy, and Purpose

 Dr. Deonne

Copyright

Dedication

For the One Who's Just Beginning to Remember

This guided journal is for the woman you're becoming,
the one who's been whispering beneath the noise,
waiting patiently for your return.

Let this be a space to listen,
to feel,
a soft place to land,
to rise,
and begin again.

–D.

And when you're ready, make it yours.

Your name

———————————————————————————

Date you began

———————————————————————————

If this book wanders, please return to

———————————————————————————

(phone number or email)

Praise for *From Tired to Inspired*

In this remarkably inviting and accessible guide, Deonne shares the lessons, practices, and gifts of her own self-recovery. If the clarity of her voice is evidence of the peace she's found, **these tools do real magic.** For anyone ready to take an honest inventory of their whole self, Deonne is a wise and kind companion.
— **Karen Faith,** Founder and CEO, Others Unlimited

There is a special light about Deonne Johnson—her passion, talent, and desire to help others. Spending time with her and **her book will be sure to inspire you in creating a more intentional and beautiful life for yourself.** This book is a gift—and there's magic in its pages.
— **Tiffany Peterson,** Top 1% Podcast Host

From Tired to Inspired is a breath of fresh air; real talk mixed with heartfelt guidance. Deonne's authentic voice shines through every page, inviting you into a conversation that's both comforting and empowering. **The reflective prompts and inviting journaling spaces made it easy for me to pause, look inward, and figure out where to begin.** It felt like Deonne was right there beside me, encouraging and reminding me I'm not alone. Trust me, buy two copies because you'll want to gift one immediately!
— **Rosina Sia Marie,** Freelance Artist & Global Instructional Design Specialist

Reading *From Tired to Inspired* felt like having coffee with a kind, wise friend. Each personal story mirrored my own life, while the beautiful exercises **gently guided me to dare to want more, dare to do more, and dare to be more.** This book is a warm embrace of understanding and encouragement. By the final page, my familiar heaviness had lifted, replaced by an unmistakable spark of possibility and hope.
— **Mindy Young,** Co-Founder, Constructive Alchemy

From Tired to Inspired is a beautiful book that helps you reconnect with yourself. Deonne Johnson's honest words and gentle guidance make you feel seen and understood. **Each chapter is like a caring hug, reminding you that you already have strength and wisdom inside.** It's about discovering what matters most and finding the courage to live your true self with kindness and confidence. This inspiring guide is perfect for anyone ready to make positive changes with clarity and courage.
— **Shelley A. Murdock,** Author & Longevity Coach

From Tired to Inspired is a breath of fresh air. Readers are invited to examine their lives with curiosity, grace, and a renewed sense of hope. This isn't a book of quick fixes or empty promises, but a sincere and honest reflection on what it means to live more intentionally, authentically, and soulfully. **This book is an invitation to pause, to breathe, to reflect—and ultimately, to rediscover the light within.** I'm so grateful for Deonne Johnson's voice and the care she put into this work. It's one I'll return to again and again.
— **Jennifer Day Walker,** Therapist, Jen Walker Therapy

What I deeply admire about Deonne is her gentle clarity. There's no fluff or filler— just genuine wisdom, offered with warmth and intention. What struck me most in this book is how practically **she guides you back to yourself,** page by page, without any pressure to perform or pretend. Her words feel like a conversation with a trusted friend: honest, insightful, and quietly transformative. If you're craving a book that will genuinely shift your perspective and support you in meaningful, everyday ways, this is the one.
— **Navreet Pabla,** Author of *If My Heart Could Talk*

I first met Deonne while digging trenches together in rural Nepal, a setting that says everything about her commitment to service, leadership, and transformation. She walks her talk. In *From Tired to Inspired*, she brings that same grounded wisdom, humor, and fierce heart to every page. **This book isn't theory, it's truth earned through experience.** It will inspire anyone who's ready to rise into the next version of themselves.
— **Melissa Schaeffer,** Retired Executive, Rewriting her next chapter

From the first page, I felt seen. As a woman who's spent years navigating both ambition and burnout, Deonne's words offered both a mirror and a balm. *From Tired to Inspired* doesn't ask you to hustle for healing; it invites you to remember your wholeness. I'll be recommending this to every woman in transition, especially those who've forgotten how much power they hold.
— **Jessica Spence,** Mortgage Agent & Author of *Living Unbreakable*

From Tired to Inspired is the kind of book that finds you when you need it most. **Deonne Johnson writes with the relatable honesty of Brené Brown and the motivating clarity of Mel Robbins.** Her words feel like truth wrapped in kindness, and every chapter offers a chance to reconnect with the parts of yourself that may have gone quiet. Deonne is a gem. Wise, warm, and real, this book is a beautiful reflection of her heart and brilliance.
— **Kimberly Ellis,** Educational Learning & Design Consultant, K.Ellis Consulting

I always thought that journaling was not for me. I couldn't really see the need to use other people's prompts or thoughts to get my own life in order. Until "From Tired To Inspired" came to my attention! Deep grace and soul infuse every page of this beautiful manuscript. And while I have done much of the inner work using some of the tools Deonne shares with us, I really needed this refresher at this time in my life. The clarity and the caring resonate from every page. **I am ready to take this new inspiration out into the world with gratitude.**
— **Teri Kingston,** Founder/Owner, Real Impact Speaking

From Tired to Inspired met me in a season of emotional and physical exhaustion and offered a way forward. Dr. Deonne's words became a lifeline, helping me rise into a life of purpose, confidence, and integrity. **Through this book, I began to reclaim my energy, my self-worth, and the woman I'm becoming**—in every area of my life.
— **Vasiti Delana,** E-learning Specialist, Fiji National University

Like an eagle soaring high, my heart is lifted through the gentle clarity and deep grace in these pages. Dr. Deonne's book guides us back to the innate knowing within our body and heart. With quiet majesty and simple, loving support, it helps us **listen deeply and come into alignment with who we truly are**—showing up in the world through our gifts, intentions, and heartfelt service. A tender, joyful path back to embodied knowing and connection.
— **Cheyenne Rivers,** Yoga Teacher & Meditation Practitioner

In a world that constantly demands our attention, slowing down to reflect can feel like a radical idea. That's what makes this journal so powerful. It offers a sacred pause, **a space to reconnect with your thoughts, feelings, and intuition.** I can see myself recommending it to friends, clients, and anyone longing to feel more at home within themselves. Thank you, Deonne, for sharing your wisdom and for creating a safe space to wander, wonder, and grow.
— **MaryAnn Walker,** Life Coach & Podcaster

This book offers **a supportive roadmap to help us embark on a journey back home to ourselves.** Deonne created a beautiful work, weaving together a path that allows our self-reflection, with tools that encourage action and examples of her own walks through this path that create connection and possibility.
— **Joana Franco,** Transformative Learning Designer & Mindfulness Coach, Utah State University

Author's Note

Dear Reader,

This is the book I longed for when I didn't know how to begin again.
Not a quick fix. Not a list of hacks.
But a companion.
A guide to walk me through the fog of feeling lost and toward something truer.
Braver. More alive.

Your circumstances may be different, but I know the feeling of waking up
inside a life that no longer fits.
From the outside, everything might look *fine*.
But inside? Something feels off. Misaligned. Heavy.
That was me.

I kept pushing through until life said, *"Stop! You can't keep going like this."*

A second divorce.
A flooded basement.
The loss of my grandfather.
An emergency hysterectomy.
All within months.

I didn't know what I wanted.
I just knew I couldn't keep living the way I had been.

So I started searching.
I read the books.
Listened to podcasts.
Attended the retreats.
I journaled. Meditated. Prayed. Cried. Danced.

And somewhere in the quiet, I began to listen—
to my inner voice,
to my body,
to the wisdom I'd forgotten I had.

This book has been percolating for more than a decade.

It was shaped by heartbreak and healing.
By breakdowns and breakthroughs.
By falling apart and learning to put myself back together, piece by piece.

It's not just a guided journal.
It's my story, woven with yours.
It's the guide I wanted, the guide I **needed**,
when I didn't know how to begin again.

I wrote this for the woman who's always been strong,
yet finally ready to be soft too.
For the woman who's accomplished so much
and still hears the whisper, *"There has to be more than this."*

You don't have to figure it all out.
You don't have to muscle your way through the sludge.

Like the lotus, your beauty isn't in avoiding the mud—
it's in rising from it.

This is your invitation to come home to yourself.
To remember what you've forgotten.
To choose you, again and again.

I'm honored to walk beside you.

With love,
Deonne

For women ready to rise, reflect, and rewrite their next chapter.

drdeonne.com

A Gift from My Heart to Yours

Every journey begins with a small step, and I want yours to begin with a gift.

This book isn't just words on a page. It's a companion. To support you beyond these pages, I've created the Transformation Toolkit, a collection of resources designed to help you deepen the practices you'll find here.

Inside the Toolkit you'll receive:

- **Printable worksheets** from this book so you can revisit them anytime
- **Guided meditations** (Loving-Kindness, Hoʻoponopono, Body Scan, and more) to bring the practices to life
- **Curated resources** to keep you inspired long after you've closed the book

Simply scan the code below or visit drdeonne.com/toolkit to access your gift.

With love,
Deonne

P.S. I'm so glad you're here.

Scan the QR code to access
your **Transformation Toolkit**
or visit drdeonne.com/toolkit

Table of Contents

What This Guide Will Help You Do

Reconnect with Your Inner Knowing
Deep down, you already have the answers. This guide helps you slow down, listen, and trust the wisdom within.

Get Clear on What Matters
Cut through the noise and reconnect with what's truly meaningful to you— not the expectations, roles, or *shoulds* that have piled up over time.

Break Free from What's Been Holding You Back
Identify the patterns, beliefs, or dynamics that are keeping you stuck—and begin to release them with compassion, not criticism.

Give Yourself Permission to Dream Bigger
It's time to stop shrinking and start expanding. You'll be invited to imagine a life that lights you up and then begin building it, one choice at a time.

Take Action That Feels Aligned, Not Overwhelming
This isn't about hustle or perfection. It's about intentional momentum. Small shifts create big transformations when they come from the inside out.

This isn't just a place to write things down.
It's a tool for coming home to yourself
and designing your next chapter with clarity, courage, and grace.

How to Use This Guide

This guide is intentionally designed to meet you where you are.

Whether you're in the thick of change, standing at a crossroads, or simply craving more alignment, this is your space to move at a pace that feels nourishing, not pressured.

There's no wrong way to use this book. Think of the following as invitations, not instructions.

Follow the Flow—or Trust Your Intuition

The chapters build on one another, but you don't have to go in order.
Start where your soul says *yes*.

Go at Your Own Pace—but Keep Going

Some days, you'll write pages. Other days, a single sentence will suffice.
Honor your rhythm. Progress over perfection.
Pause between chapters if needed. Let what rises have room to settle.
This is a journey, not a sprint.

Let It Sink In

Each section offers grounded tools and reflection prompts to help you pause,
process, and integrate, creating space for meaningful shifts to take root.

☀︎⌇ Inspired Practice

These tools help you live the work. Some will invite you to reflect on paper.
Others may simply offer a fresh perspective to carry with you as you move
through your day. Inspired Practices are small, meaningful actions that help
bridge insight and embodiment so the work doesn't just stay on the page, but
lives in your everyday life.

✎‿ Pause & Ponder

These reflection prompts help you integrate, looking gently at your thoughts,
beliefs, and experiences with kindness and curiosity. You'll find a few prompts,
followed by space to write, sketch, or simply be with what's rising.

Make It Yours

Highlight. Doodle. Journal in the margins. Dog-ear the pages.
This is your journey, let it reflect your truth and your style.

Find Your Favorite Pen

There's real power in writing by hand.
It connects you to your inner wisdom in a way typing never will.
So find a pen and choose one you love.

Set a Future Check-In

Right now, set a reminder for 90 days from today.

When it goes off, come back to this guided journal, even for five minutes.
Notice how far you've come. Recommit. Recalibrate. Reignite.

Remember This
Above all, be gentle with yourself.
Growth isn't linear. And you don't have to rush your becoming.

You're not starting over.
You're starting from experience, wisdom, and strength.

Final Thought Before We Begin

There's a phrase I want you to carry with you as you begin this journey:
What you're not changing, you're choosing.
Take a breath and read that again.

This isn't meant to shame or pressure you; it's meant to empower you.

Because if something in your life feels misaligned, heavy, or hollow,
you don't have to stay there.

You get to choose something new.
Everything in this book is something I've personally used to navigate my own
turning points.
I know the terrain.
You don't need another expert telling you what to do.
You need a guide who honors the wisdom already rising in you.

If you read these pages and don't take action, nothing will change.
But if you show up, even just a little...
If you meet just one prompt with your whole heart...
If you take one small, sacred step...

Your life will begin to shift.
Not all at once.
But moment by moment.

Choice by choice.
Page by page.

This is your invitation to remember your path,
with clarity, with courage, and with compassion.

You don't have to become someone new.
You just have to come home to yourself.

You already have everything you need.
This guided journal is simply here to help you remember.

You don't have to do this alone.
When you're ready, I'd be honored to walk alongside you. You can always find me at drdeonne.com.

ONE

Where You Are Isn't Who You Are

A Starting Point of Truth and Tender Awareness

"The wound is the place where the Light enters you."
— Rumi

Before you turn the page on this season of your life, you get to pause.
Not because something is broken or needs fixing,
but because true transformation begins with honest awareness.

Not urgency.
Not judgment.
Just the quiet truth.
This is what's real right now.

You might be carrying a hundred tiny responsibilities at once: grocery lists,
unread texts, the weight of being everything to everyone
Maybe you've been running on autopilot for so long that stopping feels
indulgent. Or unsafe. Or simply unfamiliar.
Maybe a part of you has quietly wondered, *"Is this all there is?"*

Maybe you've checked every box and still feel a little empty.
Or you've been so busy holding it all together, you've forgotten what you need.

But clarity begins in the stillness.
This chapter is an invitation to look inward,
not with critique, but with curiosity.
Think of it as a snapshot of a season of your life.
Not a label, not a verdict. Just a mirror.

Bloomprint of Life

For much of your life, you've likely focused on *doing*—checking off to-do lists, meeting deadlines, showing up for everyone else.

But when was the last time you paused to ask:
Where is my energy actually going?
Does it align with what I truly want?
And if I'm honest, do I even dare to dream?
What would I ask for if I genuinely believed it was possible?

The Bloomprint is a simple, soulful tool designed to help you see your life, not as a checklist, but as a garden.

Inspired by timeless frameworks like *Maslow's Hierarchy of Needs*, the *Wheel of Life*, and ancient wisdom traditions that honor both structure and soul, the Bloomprint blends the practical with the poetic.

It draws from the clarity of coaching, the depth of human psychology, and the sacred rhythm of nature, offering a fresh, feminine approach to growth and transformation.

Imagine a daisy in bloom.
At the center is *you*—rooted, radiant, and whole.
Each of the twelve petals represents a key area of your life.

This is your Bloomprint—a living reflection of where you are now, and where your soul is ready to grow.

There's no perfect balance to chase. No "ideal" symmetry.
Just a gentle invitation to notice, nourish, and begin again.

Each petal offers a place to explore with truth, tenderness, and curiosity.
This isn't about judgment. It's about awareness, so you can make choices that align with what matters most.

Let it be honest.
Let it be yours.
Let it bloom.

My Bloomprint Moment

The first time I mapped my Bloomprint, I thought I was doing fine.
Career thriving.
Boxes checked.
Responsibilities handled.

But when I saw it in front of me, I was surprised by what emerged.

Some areas looked strong. Others were nearly empty.

Creativity & Play? Nearly nonexistent.
Physical Vitality? Not where I wanted it to be.
Friends? Lower than I was ready to admit.

It was sobering.
Not because of what the Bloomprint revealed,
but because I had made those choices.

I had prioritized achievement and caretaking over joy, rest, and creativity.
And I'd been holding it all together for everyone else while quietly coming undone inside.

So I began to shift.
Not all at once. Just small, meaningful changes.

An hour at the piano, just for me.
Watercolor brushstrokes turned into meditation.
Stretching on my yoga mat, not to burn calories, but to come home to myself.
Curling up in a hammock without an agenda.
Sitting by the fire, letting the flames do the talking.
Saying no more often, so I could say yes to what I truly wanted.

These small actions didn't look like progress on paper,
but they *felt* like breath,
like an exhale I didn't know I'd been holding.

And over time, those small acts became a slingshot, pulling me inward just
long enough to catapult me forward.

I noticed more inspiration.
More ease.
More alignment.

Not because I was *doing* more,
but because I was finally honoring what had been missing.

The Bloomprint didn't fix my life.
But it showed me where to begin.

And that was enough.

What Each Bloomprint Petal Represents

Before you begin coloring in your Bloomprint, take a moment to explore what
each petal represents.

These descriptions provide a starting point, offering a way to reflect on each
area of your life with compassion and curiosity.
But remember, this is your Bloomprint. You get to define what each petal
means to you.

Let these be guideposts, not rules. If something feels off, rewrite it. If a word
doesn't fit, change it. Trust your own wisdom.

Work & Contribution
How aligned and fulfilled you feel in the ways you spend your time, energy, and talents—paid or unpaid.

Home & Surroundings
How supported, safe, and at ease you feel in your physical spaces—whether it's your home, car, office, or favorite corner.

Money & Finances
How empowered and at peace you feel with your financial life—from income and expenses to savings and stability.

Physical Vitality
How strong, rested, and connected you feel in your body—your energy, movement, rest, and overall well-being.

Creativity & Play
How free and joyful you feel to express, explore, and create—without pressure or perfection.

Emotional Well-Being
How tuned in and cared for you feel emotionally—your ability to feel, process, and honor your inner experience.

Friends
How connected, seen, and supported you feel by your chosen circle—those who truly see and support you.

Romantic Connection
How content or curious you feel in the realm of romantic love—whether solo, partnered, or simply exploring what love means to you.

Family
How supported and grounded you feel in your relationships—whether family of origin or family of choice.

Personal Growth
How alive and evolving you feel—whether through learning, unlearning, or becoming more fully yourself.

Spirituality

How connected you feel to the sacred—your inner peace, intuition, or a higher presence guiding and grounding you.

Legacy & Impact

How meaningful your life feels in terms of the ripple effects you're creating—through love, leadership, service, or simply by being you.

☀︎∿ Inspired Practice
Your Bloomprint

Each of the twelve petals on your Bloomprint represents a vital area of your life, from creativity and relationships to rest and purpose.

Think of each petal as a part of your life that's longing to be seen, supported, or celebrated.

Here's how to begin.
For each petal, reflect on how fulfilled you feel in that area of your life.
Then color in each petal—starting from the center and moving outward.

- A fully colored petal = high fulfillment
- A lightly shaded petal = an area that's asking for your attention
- A blank petal = a beautiful place to begin

Use one color or a rainbow of hues.
Play with color intensity to reflect your energy—bold strokes for what's blooming, soft shading for what feels tender or paused.

Colored pencils, markers, even watercolor—whatever brings you joy. Let your Bloomprint become as expressive as you are.

This is your moment of reflection and truth. Let it reflect you.

When you've completed all twelve petals, take a step back.
What emerged?
What story does it tell?

Some petals may feel full and vibrant.
Others may feel depleted or tender.
That's okay. Life is dynamic.

This isn't a performance.
It's a moment of truth.

A client permitted me to share her Bloomprint.
Let it spark curiosity, *not comparison*.
Your bloom will look different because your life *is* different.

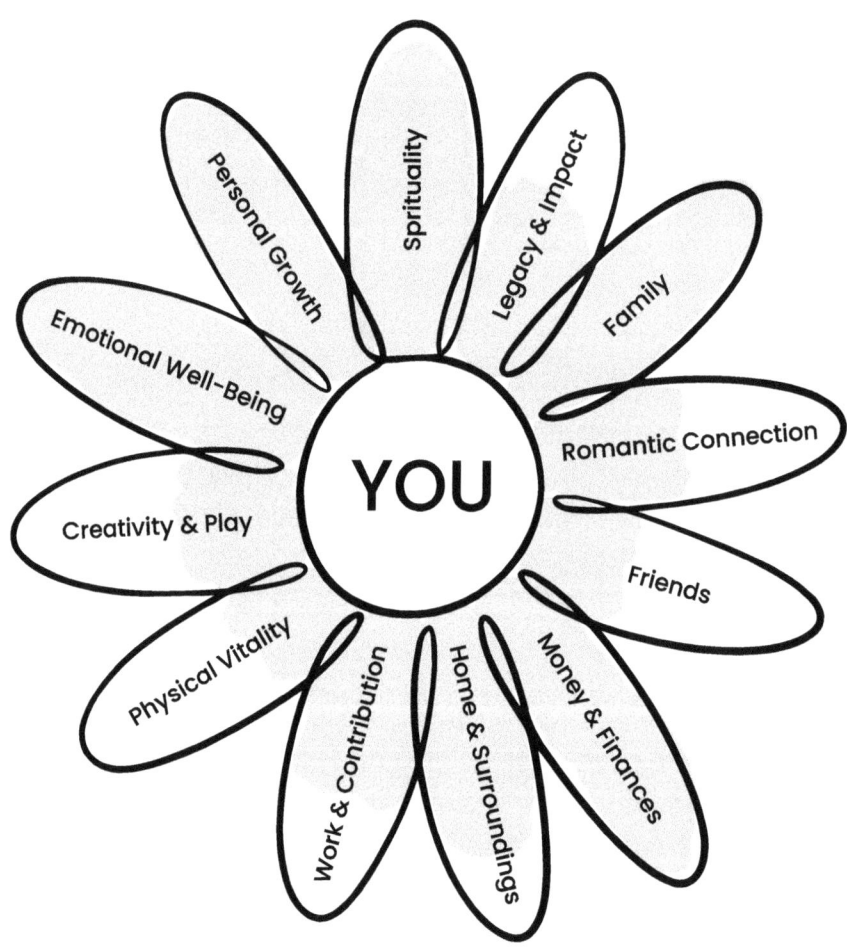

Next, you'll find a blank Bloomprint
waiting for your presence, your honesty, your awareness.

Take your time.
There's no perfect answer.

Just the courage to meet yourself as you are.
That's where clarity begins.

We'll revisit your Bloomprint later
not to judge how far you've come, but to witness what changes when you align
with your truth.

But for now?
Let's begin.

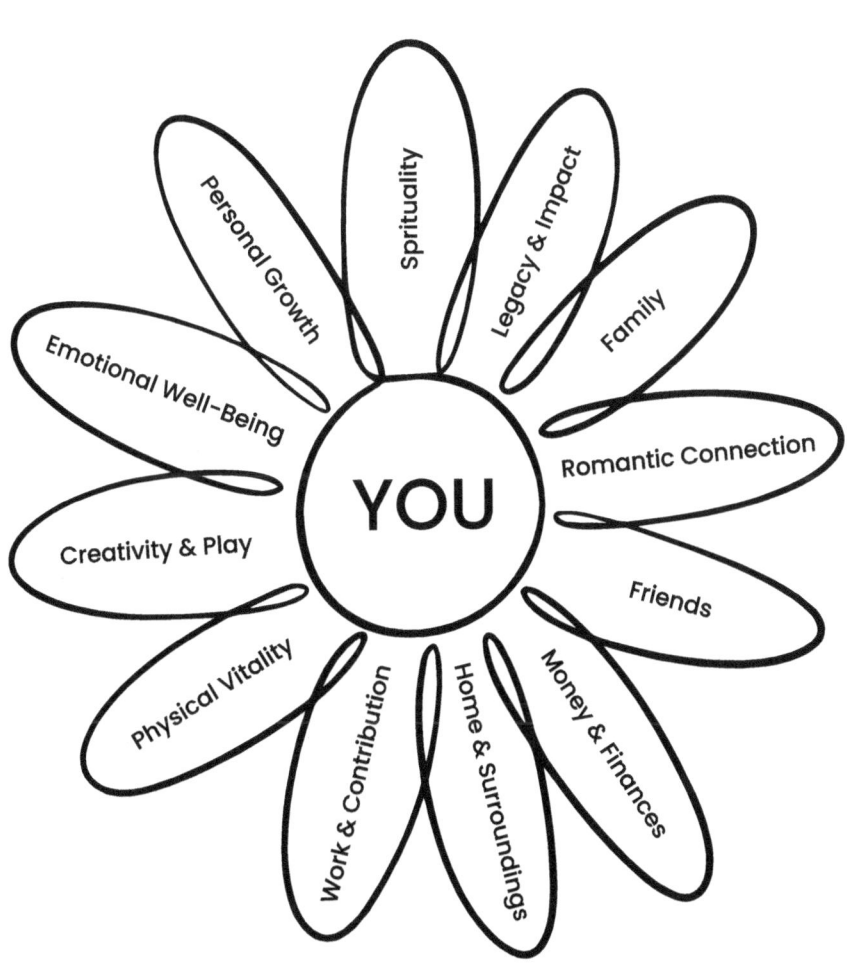

✎‿ Pause & Ponder
An Invitation to Notice and Wonder

Now that you've completed your Bloomprint, pause. Breathe.

Remember, this isn't a test.
It's a mirror. A moment. An encouragement to meet yourself with gentle honesty.

Place one hand on your heart, the other on your belly, and take a slow breath. Feel yourself arrive. Then reflect.

Let this be a soft invitation to tune inward and express outward in whatever way feels most true, using whatever tools feel most natural to you.

- Free-flow journaling
- Bullet points
- Sketches or doodles

There's no right way—only your way.

Here's a simple framework to guide your initial reflection.
— *One thing I noticed is...*
— *One thing I wonder is...*
— *One thing this might mean is...*
— *One thing I feel in my body is...*

Let your thoughts land softly.
No pressure. No fixing.
Just noticing.

✎ Pause & Ponder
What's Steady and Strong?

Begin with what's working. What feels steady, supported, even thriving.
Acknowledge it. Celebrate it. Let yourself savor and be grateful.
Use this space to reflect.
— *What areas of your life feel aligned?*
— *Where do you feel grounded, energized, or at ease?*
— *What's been helping you stay connected to these parts?*
— *What do you want to continue doing or being?*

Let this be a moment of quiet and deep celebration.
You've been doing more for yourself than you may realize.

✎ Pause & Ponder
What's Asking for Attention?

Now gently turn toward what's feeling off, not to judge, but to kindly notice.

— *What area feels neglected, stretched, or disconnected?*
— *What surprised you the most when you saw your Bloomprint?*
— *What might this part of your life be trying to say?*
— *What have you been prioritizing or maybe avoiding?*

Remember, awareness is an act of self-care.
You're not here to fix it all.
You're here to listen.

✎ Pause & Ponder
One Small Shift

Insight is powerful, especially when it creates aligned action.
— *What's one small, meaningful shift you could make this week? (Not a grand overhaul, just one nourishing move.)*
— *How might that ripple into other areas?*
— *If your Bloomprint could speak, what would it whisper to you?*

Let these answers arrive softly. No pushing. No pressure.

As you move through the rest of this book, you'll explore each petal more deeply, tending the parts of your life that are ready to grow, bloom, and be seen.

You'll return to your Bloomprint at the end of your journey. You might be surprised how much has shifted.

You've just taken the first step, and it's a powerful one. It didn't offer all the answers, but it gave you something even more valuable, awareness.
And now you can see where the tension lives.
You see what your garden's been craving.

That's the beginning of everything.

You're no longer lost in the weeds.
You're beginning to tend your garden with care.
The woman who just colored her Bloomprint?
She's not lost. She's in bloom.

You don't need to have it all figured out.
You just need to stay with yourself.

Let this be enough for now.

You've paused.
You've looked inward.
You've told the truth with tenderness.

This is how real change begins.
Not with force. With awareness.
Not with hustle. With honesty.

You're not behind.
You're becoming.

Scan the QR code to access
your **Bloomprint Worksheet**
or visit drdeonne.com/bloomprint

TWO

What Do You Actually Want?

Reclaiming Clarity, Values, and the Joy That Lights You Up

"A journey of a thousand miles begins with a single step."
— Lao Tzu

Before you design a life that feels like home, first get clear on what truly matters to *you*.

Not your boss.
Not your partner.
Not your kids.
Not the younger version of you with a different dream.
But you, here and now.

In Chapter 1, you created a snapshot of your life,
what's working, what's not, and what's quietly calling for your attention.

Awareness is powerful, but it's just the first step.

Clarity needs direction; without it, you stay stuck in the swirl.

Core Values

Values shape your life.
They influence your decisions, guide your priorities, and determine what feels fulfilling or frustrating.

And yet, most people rarely take time to deeply know and name their values, let alone live them.

When you're clear on what truly matters,
it becomes easier to say *yes* to what lights you up,
and *no* to what drains you.

**Because if everything is important,
nothing is important.**

And every time you say yes to something,
you're also saying no to something else.

This is where your core values come in.

Values give you a compass.
An anchor.
A north star.
A sacred filter for your energy and your choices.

For me, once I got clear on mine, it was like flipping a switch.
My decision-making got faster. Lighter. Aligned.

One of my core values is *adventure*.
From the outside, that might look like passports and plane tickets.
And yes, I love to travel.

But *adventure*, for me, is deeper than that.
It's about expanding my comfort zone.
It's about growth, presence, and connecting deeply with myself.
It's being fully awake, whether I'm standing on top of a mountain in Nepal or trying a new recipe on a Monday night.

When I stopped waiting for *adventure* to show up and started creating it, everything shifted.

My soul softened.
My nervous system exhaled.
(Even now, writing these words, I can feel that same exhale.)

I stopped treating *adventure* like a luxury I had to earn.
I stopped justifying it, minimizing it,
or tucking it at the bottom of the list behind everyone else's needs.

Instead, I began weaving it into my everyday life, intentionally, with presence.

And that simple shift changed the energy of everything around me.

I created space for spontaneity.
For play.
For the kind of quiet magic that shows up when you follow the spark of joy.

This chapter is an invitation to do the same.
To pause.
To quiet the noise.
And to name what actually matters to you in this season of your life.

Because here's the truth.
Most of us have inherited values without even realizing it.
We absorb what we're taught.
We repeat what's rewarded.

We say we value family, success, or service
but sometimes we're echoing what's familiar, not what's true.

And sometimes we say we value something...
but our *budget* paints another picture.
Our color-coded *calendar* whispers different priorities.
Our *energy* and *focus* reveal something else entirely.

If someone assessed your values based on where your money, time, and attention go, what would they say?

Productivity over play?
Work over rest?
Obligation over creativity?

No wonder so many of us feel drained, disconnected, and burned out.

But here's the good news, awareness changes everything.

Getting clear on your values isn't just self-awareness,
it's self-empowerment.

When you name your core values, everything begins to shift.

Decisions become easier.
Confidence grows.
Self-trust deepens.

And life begins to align—your relationships, your schedule, your choices start
to reflect what actually matters.

You stop chasing what looks good on paper
and start creating what feels right in your heart.

You say *yes* to what's aligned.
You say *no*—with less guilt, and way less drama.

You realize...
You don't need more discipline.
You just need more clarity.

That's what values do.
They bring you home to yourself.

So here's your invitation.
In a world that pulls you in every direction and tells you what should matter,
listen inward.

Your values are the quiet truths that guide how you live, love, and lead.
Getting clear on them will not only change how you make decisions,
but it will also change how you move through the world.

☀〰 Inspired Practice
Begin With What's Real

Now it's time to tune in and discover what truly matters to *you*.

Not what looks good on paper.
Not what's been expected.
Not what someone else once told you *should* matter.

But what's real.
Right now.
In *this* season of your life.

Let's begin by slowing down, tuning in,
and letting your values rise to the surface.

Step 1: Start with a Spark
Scan the list of values on the next page.
Don't overthink it, let your body and intuition lead.

Place a **small dot** next to every word that resonates, stirs something in you, or simply feels important.
There's no limit.
Dot as many as you'd like.

Step 2: Narrow It Down
Take a deep breath.
Now, look back over your dotted values and **underline 10–15** that feel most meaningful.

You might notice themes.
You might surprise yourself.

There's no need to be perfect, just honest.
Let it be part of the process.

Step 3: Choose Your Three

From your underlined list, **circle your top three**, the ones that feel essential to how you want to live.

These are your *anchors*.
The principles that steady you when things feel chaotic.
The lens you reach for when a decision feels hard.

If this part feels tricky, you're not alone.
It's not about getting it *right*; it's about telling the truth.

And remember, you can always come back and refine.

Tip:

If you notice similar values (Love, Belonging, and Connection), group them.
Let the patterns reveal themselves.
Then choose one word from each group that feels most essential, most *you*.

There's no correct answer, only what's *real* for you.

Core Values List

Accountability	Family	Nature
Achievement	Flexibility	Nurturing
Adaptability	Flow	Openness
Adventure	Forgiveness	Optimism
Alignment	Freedom	Order
Authenticity	Friendship	Ownership
Awareness	Fulfillment	Partnership
Balance	Fun	Patience
Belonging	Generosity	Play
Boundaries	Gentleness	Peace
Bravery	Grace	Presence
Calm	Gratitude	Prosperity
Clarity	Growth	Purpose
Collaboration	Happiness	Receiving
Community	Harmony	Reflection
Compassion	Healing	Recognition
Confidence	Health	Resilience
Connection	Honesty	Respect
Consistency	Hope	Responsibility
Contentment	Humility	Rest
Contribution	Humor	Safety
Courage	Independence	Security
Creativity	Inner Peace	Self-Compassion
Curiosity	Integrity	Self-Expression
Depth	Intuition	Self-Respect
Devotion	Joy	Service
Dignity	Justice	Simplicity
Discipline	Kindness	Spirituality
Empathy	Knowledge	Stability
Empowerment	Leadership	Success
Encouragement	Learning	Trust
Equality	Listening	Truth
Equity	Love	Understanding
Excellence	Loyalty	Wholeness
Faith	Mindfulness	Wisdom
Fairness	Meaningful Work	Other:

✎ Pause & Ponder
What's True for You?

Now that you've named your values, pause.
Take a deep breath.
Let them settle into your body.
Let them live in your choices, in your daily rhythm.

Ask yourself:
— *Which of these values feel like familiar truths?*
— *Which ones surprised you?*
— *Where did you hesitate or feel torn? Why?*
— *How do these three values reflect who you are in this season of life?*

Let this be a check-in with your inner compass. There's no perfect set of values, only what's real for *you* right now.

✎ Pause & Ponder
Define What Matters

Take a moment to define each of your top values in your own words.
— *What does this value look like in your life?*
— *What deeper need does it meet?*
— *What does it feel like when it's present or when it's missing?*

Here's what that looks like in my life.

Value: *Adventure*

For me, *adventure* means leaning into the unknown with open hands and an open heart. It meets my deeper need for expansion, curiosity, and aliveness. When it's present, I feel awake, connected, and fully myself—like the edges of my life are stretching just wide enough to let in possibility.
When it's missing, I often feel stuck. Small. Like I'm living on repeat instead of writing a story that excites me.

Value #1: _____
— *What does this value look like in your life?*
— *What deeper need does it meet?*
— *What does it feel like when it's present—or when it's missing?*

Value #2: _____

— *What does this value look like in your life?*
— *What deeper need does it meet?*
— *What does it feel like when it's present—or when it's missing?*

Value #3 _____

— *What does this value look like in your life?*
— *What deeper need does it meet?*
— *What does it feel like when it's present—or when it's missing?*

Values in Action

You've named your values and defined them.
Now comes the hard part, *living* them.

It's evaluating whether your resources—your money, time, and attention—are truly honoring those values.

When I realized that *adventure* was one of my core values, I had to ask myself—
Am I actually living this out, or just wishing I was?
Am I blocking off time for it?
Making decisions around it?
Prioritizing it in the way I say it matters?

It wasn't about perfection—it was about *alignment*.
And alignment brings ease.

☀︎〰 Inspired Practice
Charting Your Values

On this page, you'll see a completed chart, showing an example of how this exercise works.

On the next page, and you'll find a blank chart waiting for you. This is your space to create a visual snapshot of how aligned your life is with your values.

This isn't about budgeting every dollar or tracking every minute.
It's about checking in, *honestly*, with how well your life is supporting what truly matters.

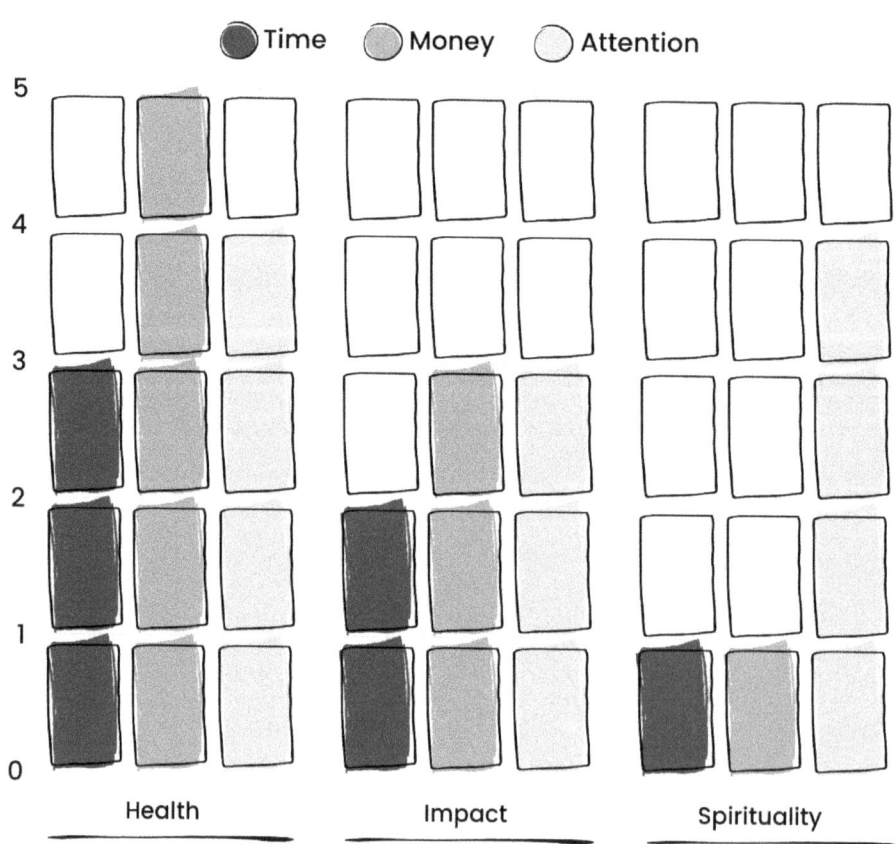

Instructions:
For your top three values, rate each from 1 (not aligned) to 5 (fully aligned).

Money: Are you comfortable with what you're investing here?
Time: Are you spending it in ways that reflect this value?
Attention: Are you giving it your focus, your heart, your presence?

Create a visual snapshot—let the bars tell a story. They'll reveal where your life feels supported and where something may need to shift.

Make this your own. Use colors, patterns, or styles to fill in your legend. Get creative—dots, stripes, shading, or whatever feels natural. Alignment isn't about perfection; it's about clarity.

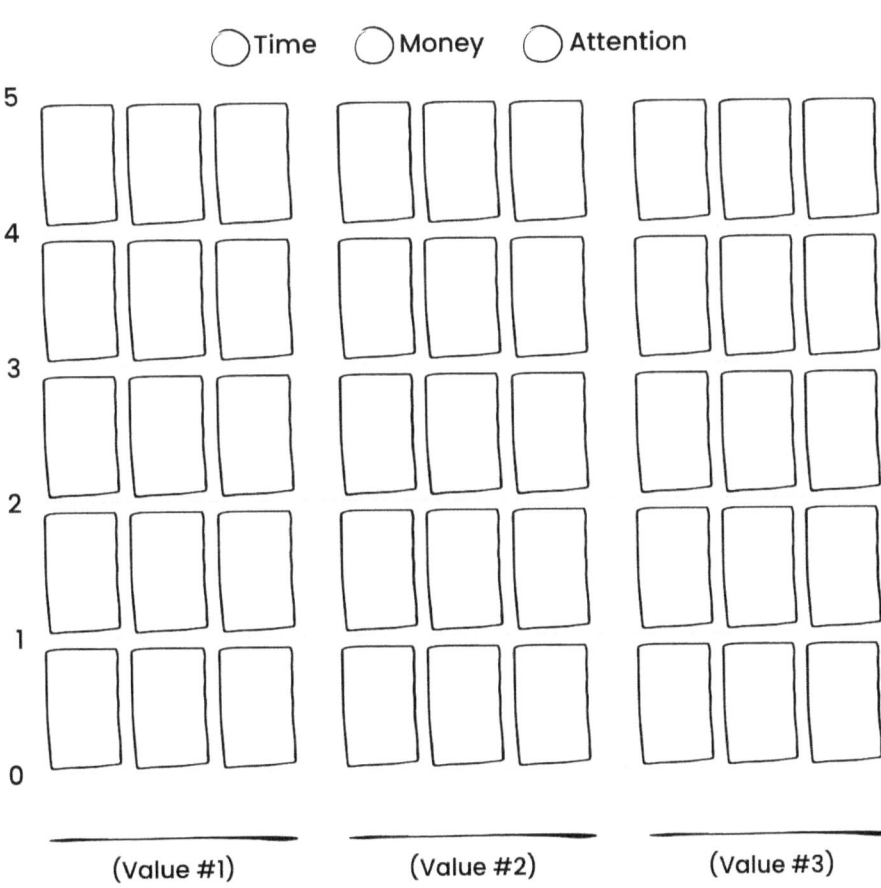

Charting Your Values

◯Time   ◯Money   ◯Attention

(Value #1)   (Value #2)   (Value #3)

✎⌒ Pause & Ponder
What's Aligned? What's Asking for More?

Let your truth speak.
— *Which value feels most fully supported in your life right now? What's helping to make that happen?*
— *Which value feels out of sync? What might be getting in the way?*
— *Is there a slight shift—of time, money, or energy—you're curious to try?*

Let this be a moment of clarity, not to criticize, but to notice where your inner and outer lives are whispering for deeper alignment.

Values aren't fixed.
They're dynamic, living truths that grow and shift as you do.

What matters to you now might not be what mattered five years ago, or even five months ago.
And that's okay. That's wisdom. That's evolution.

Revisiting your values regularly, on your birthday, on New Year's Day, or after a big life change, can be a beautiful gift to yourself.
A sacred check-in. A way to honor who you're becoming.

Some values will stay steady, like anchors in a storm.
Others may rise unexpectedly, asking to be seen, named, and honored.

Either way, returning to this practice is a reminder that your life deserves to be lived in alignment, with clarity, intention, and joy.

Joy List

This isn't about rearranging your entire life overnight.
It's about noticing what's ready to change and choosing to respond.

Alignment isn't about being perfect.
It's about being *honest*.
And honest alignment is the beginning of freedom.

By now, you've named what matters to you.
You've looked at how well you're *living* those values in real time.
Now let's drop into something even deeper.

What brings you joy?

There was a season in my life when I had everything "together."
But I couldn't remember the last time I felt lit up from the inside.

So I made a different kind of list.

Not a to-do list.
A *joy* list.

I sat down and asked myself:
What makes me smile without trying?
What feels like an exhale?
What fills me up, even when I'm tired?

And you know what?
Most of those things didn't cost a dime.

- Singing in my car with Diana Krall, sunroof open, seat warmers on, volume up
- Sharing a meal with people I love, deep conversation filling the space
- Swinging in a hammock in the woods, a good book and snack at the ready
- Offering random acts of kindness, doing something for someone without expecting anything in return
- Playing my grand piano late at night, just me and Beethoven
- Journaling with a cup of tea
- Traveling somewhere new, stepping into the unknown with curiosity and wonder
- Watching the flames dance in the fire pit, wrapped in a blanket under a full moon
- Listening to live music, especially acoustic guitar *(bonus if it's one of my kids playing!)*
- Collecting office supplies *(yes, really)*—a fresh journal and my favorite pens still make me giddy

Each time I return to this practice, I remember something essential—
I *thrive* on connection.
I *need* nature.
I *crave* music and creativity.

When I don't make space for these things, I feel off.
So I come back to this list.
Not as another task, but as a way to remember who I am.

☀︎〰 Inspired Practice
Joy List

This isn't just an exercise.
It's a *practice*.
It's a way to make sure that joy isn't just an afterthought, but a way of living.

And here's something important to remember—
You don't have to get it all down right now.

This is a *living* list.
You can come back to it anytime, when you're feeling stuck, stretched, or simply in need of a bit of light.

Dog-ear this page.
Mark it with a sticky note.
Bookmark it in whatever way works for you.

Let this be a resource you return to again and again.
Because joy isn't just a feeling—it's a *remembering*.
It's a way back to who you really are.

There's no one right way to do this.

You might **write**.
You might **draw**.
You might **cut images** from a magazine.
You might **collage it, color it,** and come back to it with fresh eyes in a week.

Use the next few pages however you like.
There are no rules here, only invitations.

Capture what lights you up.

What makes you feel *alive, grounded, playful, or fully you?*

Here are a few prompts to spark your creativity.
— *What would I do if I had one free hour today?*
— *What activities make me lose track of time?*

— *What sights, sounds, or smells bring me comfort or delight?*
— *What did I love doing as a child?*
— *What kind of beauty moves me?*

Let this be a guide back to what makes you feel most alive.
You don't have to earn it.
You just get to *allow* it.

Remember, use these pages however you like—write, doodle, list, draw. Come back anytime.

Let Your Joy Flow

✎ Pause & Ponder
Joy Is a Compass

Let joy point the way.

— *What's something small that brings you joy and how can you make more space for it this week?*

— *Which items on your list surprised you? Which ones have been missing lately?*

— *When you imagine a joy-filled day, what does it look and feel like?*

— *If joy were your compass, not productivity or obligation, how might your days look, feel, or flow differently?*

You've done powerful work in this chapter.
You've named what matters.
You've gotten honest about where your money, time, and attention are going.
And you've created a personal inventory of what brings you joy, not someday, but now.

This is your foundation.
Clarity creates alignment.
And alignment creates momentum.

As you step into the next chapter, carry this with you.
You're allowed to prioritize what lights you up.
You're allowed to say no to what drains you.
You're allowed to build a life that reflects who you really are.

Let your **values** lead.
Let **joy** be your compass.
And let your next chapter rise from that sacred place inside you, the one that's always known the way.

Scan the QR code to access
your **Core Values Pack**
or visit drdeonne.com/values

THREE

Release to Receive

Letting Go of What No Longer Serves You

"Some of us think holding on makes us strong, but sometimes it is letting go."
— Hermann Hesse

You might know the feeling.
Opening a drawer that won't close.
Scrolling through your calendar and seeing nothing that feels nourishing.
Relationships that once felt comforting but now feel heavy.

We carry more than we realize, physically, mentally, and emotionally.
And sometimes, the heaviest weight is the story that says, *"I should be able to handle this."*

Before new things can grow, something has to be cleared.
A field must be tilled. A closet emptied. A belief released.

Clarity isn't just about knowing what you want;
it's about being brave enough to release what you don't.

And sometimes? That means letting go of things you've been carrying for years.

Not just the physical clutter, but the emotional weight.
The outdated roles. The self-talk that shrinks you.
The just-in-case clothes, the just-in-case relationships, the just-in-case version of you.

I was leading a humanitarian expedition to Kenya when I had a major epiphany, right in the middle of a Tai Chi flow on the savannah.
The instructor invited everyone, "Let it go."

And that's when it hit me.
I'd been carrying sh*t I thought was mine—beliefs that no longer served me, relationships that dimmed my light, old shame.

I thought being strong meant holding it quietly.
Not spreading it around. Not burdening anyone else. Not letting it show.

But in that wide-open space, a new thought emerged—
What if the Earth actually needs what I'm releasing?
What if letting go isn't burdensome—but sacred?
*What if my sh*t was actually fertilizer, something the Earth could receive, digest, and transform into beauty?*

We exhale carbon dioxide, and the trees transform it into life.
Maybe the stories, the stuff, and the shame don't have to be buried within us.
Maybe they're ready to be composted into something new.
Maybe the Earth already knows how to take what we release
and return it as something nourishing.

This isn't about throwing everything away or starting from scratch.
It's about loosening your grip on what feels heavy, not aligned.
It's about creating just enough space for something else to land,
something lighter. Truer. Freer.

Let that truth settle.

You don't have to let go of everything right now.
But maybe—just for a moment—you can imagine what it would feel like to no longer carry what's been weighing you down.

Release just one thing. One unhelpful memory. One old version of you.

Let it rest. Let it return to the earth. Let it become something else.

We often think we're holding on to a thing.
But more often, we're holding on to what that thing represents.

A memory that we believe defines who we are.
A fear of what we might lose if we finally let go.
An identity someone else gave us that we're still trying to wear.

Sometimes it's the dress we're not ready to donate... because it reminds us of a day we felt beautiful.
Or maybe it's the arts and craft drawer (or closet, or room)... because we might start, or finally finish, that project.

Realize there's often a story underneath.
You might need this someday.
You can't afford to waste it.
Don't be ungrateful.

So we save it. We store it.
We move it from house to house, season to season.
And we tell ourselves, *"It's no big deal."*

But it is.

Because those things?
They're not just taking up space on a shelf.
They're taking up space in our energy. In our decisions. In our capacity to rest.

I was raised to be resourceful and responsible.
To keep what might be useful.
To never waste.
To hope for the best and prepare for the worst.

And there was wisdom in that.
It came from ancestors who survived wars, recessions, depressions, and scarcity.

At some point, I realized, I wasn't storing supplies—I was storing fear.

Fear of not having enough.
Fear of needing what I'd just released.
Fear of regretting the choice to let go.

And that fear wasn't keeping me safe.
It was keeping me stuck.

Sometimes we hold on to something because we don't want to offend the person who gave it to us.
Or because we spent money on it, and letting it go feels wasteful.
Or because it reminds us of who we used to be, and we're not quite sure of who we're becoming.

But what if letting go isn't an act of rejection?
What if it's an act of reverence?
Of generosity?
Of surrender?
Of trust?

What if passing it on blesses someone else?
What if your release becomes someone else's relief?

Decluttering doesn't betray your past; it blesses your future.

Make Space for Magic

Letting go isn't always a dramatic act.
Sometimes it starts with a drawer.

A shelf.
A pile.
A quiet *enough is enough* whispered
while standing in the middle of your own life.

I didn't set out to transform everything.
At first, I just wanted less noise.
Less mess.
Less emotional weight staring at me from every countertop and nightstand.

So I began where I was, my closet.

Inspired by the KonMari method, I decluttered by category, not room by room.
I gathered every piece of clothing I owned from every drawer, bin, and closet.

Then, one by one, I picked up each item and asked the simplest question...
Do I love this?

Not...
Does it fit?
Could I use it someday?
Did someone I care about give this to me?

Just...
Do I love it?

Some things made me smile.
Others made me shrink.
Some belonged to a version of me I was ready to release, the woman who tried to be good, or impressive, invincible... or invisible.

There were jeans I was keeping *just in case I lost the weight.*
A bag that whispered status, but never felt like mine.
A jacket I bought because it was 70% off, not because I loved it.
And a dress I never wore, always tucked away, waiting to be chosen.

I made four piles.
Keep. Donate. Sell. Toss.

And here's what I noticed...
With every decision, I felt lighter.
Not just in my closet, but in my body.
My mind.

My heart.
My nervous system.

What changed everything for me was the story I started telling about letting go.
I stopped thinking of it as getting rid of something.
I began to see each item as a blessing that had served its purpose.

And by passing it on, it could bless someone else's life.
If I didn't love it anymore, maybe someone else would.

That shift, from guilt to generosity, made everything easier.
Even with sentimental items.
Even the *almost* and *someday* items.

Letting go also taught me what my time was worth.

I stopped posting $5 items online because it wasn't worth the time and energy.
I stopped saving things that might be useful *someday*.
I stopped negotiating with my own joy.

It took six months to thoroughly declutter my home.
And when I finished, I woke up one morning and knew—
This house is no longer mine.

I didn't clean. I didn't stage.
I took a few pictures and listed it for sale.

Within 24 hours, I bought a new home and sold my old one,
both for-sale-by-owner,
both with surprising ease.

Because the clearing had already happened.
Energetically. Emotionally. Spiritually.

That's the power of making space.
It doesn't just change your home.
It changes your life.

✎ Pause & Ponder
The Shift Begins

Let this be your clearing. A chance to loosen your grip.
To look gently at what's been weighing you down and why.
— *What are you still holding on to "just in case"?*
— *What fears or beliefs might be hiding in your closets, calendar, or cupboards?*
— *What space in your life feels most cluttered, and what might be possible if it felt light, free, or sacred?*

☀︎〰 Inspired Practice
Keep What You Love

Choose **one category**, not a room.
Clothes. Books. Paper. "Someday" items.

Pull everything out. Put it in one place.
Touch each item and ask yourself:
Do I love this?
Is this aligned with who I'm becoming?

If the answer is no, release it.
Bless it.
Donate it.
Gift it.
Let it move on.

This isn't about organizing or tidying.
It's about making space for what supports who you are becoming.

As you sort, take a photo or sketch what you see.
The pile. The process. The before and after.

Let it be a visual snapshot of your sacred unmaking.
A threshold you chose to cross.

Use the next page to doodle, reflect, or tape in your before-and-after photos.
This isn't about perfection.
It's about progress.
And most of all, it's about presence.

Let this be your proof.
You are capable of clearing what no longer serves you.
And every time you do, you're creating space for something better.

Let Go of the Old Stories

Not everything we carry lives on a shelf.

Some things live in the back of our minds.
In the roles we didn't choose.
In the ache we've normalized.
In the expectations we never agreed to.
In the identities we wear out of habit instead of truth.

Letting go isn't just about stuff.
It's about *stories*.

The story that says you have to do it all.
The one that says you missed your chance.
The story that says joy, adventure, and purpose are for someone else.
The one that says you're only worthy when you're giving, producing, or achieving.

But here's the quiet truth you already know,
You don't have to keep carrying it.

Letting go, in that sense, is holy.
It's not a rejection.
It's a return.

You are choosing, moment by moment, to become more fully yourself.

And sometimes, that choice begins with something as simple as...
making the bed.

There's a phrase I love:
"How you do one thing is how you do everything."

That small act each morning isn't about tidy sheets.
It's a ritual. A reverent gesture.
A way of saying, *"I'll take care of what I've been given.*
I'll nurture what's already mine."

Not from perfectionism, but from presence.
Not from obligation, but from devotion.

This is the sacred rhythm of the Divine Feminine.
Give us a house, we create a home.
Give us a seed, we grow a child.
Give us the mess, we turn it into a message.

But what about the one doing all the tending?
The woman showing up, smoothing corners, holding it all together?

She needs care, too.

Taking care of what you've been given includes taking care of *you*.

And that begins, not with a to-do list, but with a mirror.

✎ Pause & Ponder
What Wants to Be Released?

This is a sacred goodbye.

— *What story, role, or identity feels outdated but familiar?*
— *What beliefs have I inherited that no longer fit or serve my truest self?*
— *If I released this, what would I have space for?*

Mirror Work

We spend so much of our lives looking outside ourselves for love, validation, and approval. But real healing? *It begins within.*

Mirror work is a deceptively simple practice. You stand in front of a mirror, look yourself in the eyes, and speak to yourself with love.

And if that sounds uncomfortable, you're not alone.
Most people find it incredibly vulnerable at first.

Why?
Because the mirror reflects everything, including the parts we've been avoiding.
And the voice we use with ourselves often isn't the kindest.

Here's the truth.
When you can meet your own gaze with love, you stop needing to prove your worth to anyone else.

This practice is about softening judgment.
Building self-trust.
Remembering that you are already enough, *right here, as you are.*

There was a time in my life when I looked in the mirror and didn't think much at all.
I wasn't critical, but I wasn't loving either.
Just... neutral. Detached. Going through the motions. Hair. Makeup. Out the door.

Then, during a workshop, I was introduced to Louise Hay's mirror work.
It sounded simple. Look in the mirror and say, *"I love you."*

The facilitator invited us to stand in front of a mirror, look into our own eyes, and say, *"I love you."* Simple, right?

Except when I tried it later that night, alone in the bathroom of a friend's house, I couldn't do it.
I couldn't look myself in the eyes and say I loved myself.
That realization cracked something open.

Little by little, I began speaking to myself more.
I noticed the tension. The tightness. The expectations I didn't even realize I was carrying.

And little by little, I softened.

I began to see myself, not just the polished version I presented to the world, but the vulnerable woman beneath the mask.

Eventually, I got to a place where I could stand in front of the mirror with nothing to hide, *literally* and emotionally.

And while I may not share the full details of that journey here, I will say this—

It changed everything.

Now I smile when I look in the mirror.
(And I actually just smiled as I wrote that sentence.)

Not every day. Not perfectly.
But there's love there.
There's tremendous gratitude.

For the body that's carried me.
For the storms I've weathered.
For the self I'm learning to honor, more fully, more gently, every day.

Because once you can love yourself in the mirror, you stop looking for proof of your worth everywhere else.
You begin to feel whole in your own presence.
You begin to come home to yourself.

☀︎〜 Inspired Practice
Mirror Moments

Find a quiet moment.
Stand in front of the mirror.
Look into your own eyes.

Not to fix. Not to critique.
Just... to *be* with yourself.

If it feels safe, try saying something kind:

I see you.
I'm learning to love you.
Thank you for carrying me this far.
You're allowed to rest.
You are enough, right now.

If those feel out of reach, try this:

I'm willing to learn how to love you.
I'm listening.
You matter.

Let the practice be gentle.
Let it evolve.
Let it be yours.

Use the next page to write a note to yourself.
A phrase. A letter. A whisper of compassion.

Let this be your mirror.
Let this be your truth.

✏️ Pause & Ponder
In the Mirror

Meet yourself with gentle eyes.
— *When I meet my own gaze, what do I see?*
— *What am I learning to love about myself, right now, as I am?*

☀〰 Inspired Practice
Let It Go, Let It Grow

This is your invitation to release—gently, honestly, fully.

Not to judge what's been carried, but to name it with compassion.
Not to fix anything, but to clear space for something new.

Here's how to begin.
Use a separate sheet of paper, something outside of these pages.
This isn't for reflection. It's for release.
Let it be raw. Let it be real.

Ask yourself—boldly, softly:
— *What am I still holding on to out of fear, guilt, or obligation?*
— *What belief, expectation, or identity no longer feels true?*
— *What version of myself is ready to be released?*
— *Who might I become without this weight?*

Write it down, scribbles or sentences, symbols or shapes.
Let it out of your body. Let it live on the page.
And when it feels complete, let it go.

Burn it.
Shred it.
Tear it up.
Bury it beneath a tree.
Release it with intention and reverence.

This is your sacred goodbye.

Not to erase what was,
but to choose what comes next.

You've carried it long enough.
Now, you let it go.
Let this be your exhale.

You've just done some of the most important work of this journey,
not by adding more,
but by *releasing* what no longer serves you.

You've cleared space in your home, your heart, and your mind.
And that space?
It's not emptiness.
It's sacred.
It's an invitation.
It's the quiet hum of possibility returning.

What comes next is just as powerful—
Choosing what to welcome in.

Because once you've cleared the noise,
you can finally hear your desires.
Not the ones the world told you to want,
but the ones that have always lived inside you.

FOUR

Calm the Noise, Hear Your Truth

Rewriting the Stories So Your Soul Can Speak

"When you change the way you look at things, the things you look at change."
— Wayne Dyer

There comes a point in every woman's becoming
when the old mental soundtrack, the one that helped her survive,
starts getting in the way of the life she's here to create.

Not because she's failing.
Not because she's broken.
But because those old thought patterns were built for a different chapter,
and she's already turned the page.

Maybe you know that feeling.
The inner critic that won't go quiet.
The "what-ifs" that steal your sleep.
The looped story that keeps telling you to play it safe, stay small, or wait your
turn. But the truth? You were meant to shine.

Your mind has been trying to protect you.
That's the power of your limbic brain; it keeps you alive.
It tells stories to make sense of your world, to avoid pain, to predict what might go wrong.

And it's done its job well.
It means well, but it doesn't always tell the truth.

This chapter isn't about shutting down your thoughts.
It's about tending to them with *compassion*.
Getting curious about the ones that feel weighty.
Releasing the ones that no longer fit.
And replacing them with something truer, softer, and more supportive of who you're becoming.

Because when the mental noise quiets down, your soul can finally speak.

Rewrite Your Story

One of the most transformative practices I've learned is inspired by Byron Katie's method of questioning painful thoughts.
It's simple, but not always easy.

When a thought feels *heavy, anxious, or quietly critical*, I ask myself:
Is it true?
Who would I be without this thought?

And then, I get curious.
Curious about what this thought is trying to protect.
Curious about the story beneath the story.

Because curiosity isn't criticism—it's kindness.
And when I meet my thoughts with compassion instead of control, I often uncover something softer.
Something more honest.
Something that helps me heal.

The first time I practiced this, I was worried about my teenage son.
The thought looping through my mind: *He's not living up to his potential.*

It felt true. Was he applying himself academically? Making healthy choices?
Choosing good friends?

But underneath that thought lived fear. Disappointment. Control.

So I paused.

Is it true?
No.

When I believed that thought, I was tense. Critical. Emotionally distant.
I was parenting from fear, not love.

And who would I be without that thought?
Without it, I could just love him. No pressure. Just presence.
Unconditional love.

And when I got curious and looked inward,
I realized it wasn't really about him. It was about me.
I wasn't living up to my potential.

That moment brought me back to myself, with softness.
With grace.
With the knowing that maybe I was the one needing more love, more trust,
more acceptance.

I've come back to this practice again and again.
Not to shame myself, but to stay rooted in love.
For myself. And for others.

Sometimes, often, it's not our own behavior we're questioning.
It's someone else's.

That friend is so flaky.
My partner never listens.
My boss doesn't value me.

My parents don't respect me.
They should be more grateful.
Why are they judging me?

Sound familiar?

But when you pause, when we gently walk those thoughts through the questions, something radical happens.
Judgment becomes a mirror.
And underneath each thought?
A part of you is asking to be seen, understood, or healed.

☀〰 Inspired Practice
Rewrite the Thought, Reclaim Your Truth

Bring a thought that's been looping in your mind.
One that feels heavy, harsh, or constricting in your body.

Write it down.

Then gently walk it through the questions.
— *Is it true?*
— *Who would I be without this thought?*
— *If I turned inward, what might I learn?*

You don't need to get it perfect.
You don't even need to believe it'll work.

Let this be a beginning. Bring your thoughts to the page and begin.

Use this space to expand, reflect, or revisit what emerged.

That Which You Permit, You Promote

The stories we carry don't just live in our heads; they show up in our choices, our boundaries, and what we allow.
Here's a truth that changed everything for me—
That which you permit, you promote.

I don't say that with shame or blame, I say it with power.

There was a time I found myself tolerating behavior that didn't align with my core values,
accepting less than I deserved,
making excuses for what I knew didn't feel right,
calling it "love" or "patience" or "compassion"
when it was really *fear.*

And when I finally stopped pointing outward
and looked at my own side of the fence,
I realized, *I wasn't just allowing it. I was affirming it.*

It reminds me of something I heard from Mel Robbins. She calls it the "Let Them" theory. And it's as simple and powerful as it sounds.

Let them.
Let them judge you.
Let them ignore you.
Let them take the low road.
Let them misunderstand you.

You don't get to control anyone else.
You only get to choose how you show up.

And here's where the deeper work begins.

Let me.
Let me rest.
Let me say no.
Let me grow, *without guilt.*

When people show you who they are, believe them.
And when you keep tolerating behavior that hurts you, remember—
That which you permit, you promote.

Let them.
Let me.
That shift changed everything.

The more I practiced this, the more I realized how many inner voices I had given power to *without ever agreeing to their terms.*

Some were loud and critical.
Others were quiet but persistent.

And one day, I pictured them all sitting around a large conference table, offering their very opinionated opinions.

That's when I realized, it was time to call a meeting.

Voices at the Table

One of the most impactful metaphors I've embraced is what I call **Voices at the Table**. I first heard a version of this concept from Wayne Dyer years ago, and it helped me reclaim my rightful seat at the head of the table.

Imagine this:
Your mind is a boardroom.
A table surrounded by voices, some kind, some critical.
Some familiar. Some inherited.

A former teacher.
An ex.
A parent who meant well but missed the mark.
A boss who never saw your brilliance.
Maybe even a younger version of yourself, still scared, still trying to earn her place.

You didn't choose all those voices.
But you *can* choose who stays.

When I looked around my boardroom, I realized I was still giving my former manager a seat.
And, harder still, I saw my mother sitting there, too.

Her voice wasn't cruel. But it didn't offer a soft landing.
It was heavy with expectation.
Heavy with silence.
Heavy with the weight of things I was asked to carry.

I longed for closeness, but her walls were high and well-guarded.
And for too long, I believed her distance meant something was wrong with me.
Somewhere along the way, I confused self-worth with performance.

I've forgiven her in many ways.
I can see now—she was doing the best she could, with what she had, from where she came from.
But that doesn't mean her voice gets to stay.

So I did something that felt both radical and right.
I thanked her for all she taught me, for the love she tried to give in her own way.
And then, with love and clarity, I ushered her out.

Because this boardroom is mine.
And I need *my* voice at the head of the table.

Now?
It's filled with wise women.
With cheerleaders. Thought leaders. Future versions of me.
With the part of me that trusts divine timing.
That values play.
That no longer performs to prove her worth.

This is the inner council I choose to let lead.
Not fear. Not guilt. Not inherited expectations.
But clarity. Compassion. Courage.

☀︎〰 Inspired Practice
Who Sits at Your Table Now?

You've met the voices that once shaped your inner dialogue.
Now it's time to invite in the ones that serve your becoming.

Use this space to sketch, list, or describe who gets a seat at your table now.
The kind, wise, intuitive parts of you.
The mentors, inner guides, and future selves who hold your vision with love.

There's no right way to do this.
Just let your inner council take shape, seat by seat, voice by voice.
And most importantly, **put yourself at the head of the table.**

It's ready for a new meeting.
And the woman who gets to call that meeting to order **is you.**

Who sits at your table now? Let your vision take shape.

✎⌒ Pause & Ponder
Release and Reframe

Before you answer, pause. Feel it in your body. Let the first answer arise, not the "right" one.
Be honest. Be kind. Be curious.
Let this be a gentle moment of reflection, an invitation to release what no longer fits and to begin writing a new story.

What thought or belief have you been carrying that feels outdated or unkind?

Let it rise without judgment. It might sound like, "I'm too much," or "I have to do it all myself."
For me, one belief that surfaced was: "If I don't hold it all together, everything will fall apart." It was a dense thought, one I carried quietly for years.

Where do you sense it came from?

A message from childhood? A role you played for too long? Something you absorbed from culture, work, or a past relationship?
Mine was rooted in childhood, shaped by being the "good one." I was the fixer before I even had the words to name it.

What was this belief trying to protect you from?

Even if it no longer serves you, can you honor how it helped you survive, belong, or stay safe?
My belief helped me feel useful. Capable. In control. It protected me from being hurt.

How is it holding you back now?

What is it costing you—emotionally, mentally, or relationally?
It kept me from asking for help, from resting, from letting others show up for me.

What do you want to believe instead?

What thought would feel more true, more loving, more you?
Now, I'm practicing: "It's safe to let go. I don't have to hold it all." It still feels unfamiliar, uncomfortable, and yet incredibly freeing.

If you lived from this new belief, how might your day look different?
How would you speak to yourself? What choices might you make?
I'd pause more. Breathe deeper. Say yes to support. I'd speak to myself like someone I love.

Let your answers arrive softly.
You don't have to get it right. You just have to be real.

This is how you begin to rewrite the story, with grace, not force.

You've done something powerful in this chapter.

You've listened to the thoughts that swirl beneath the surface,
not to silence them, but to understand them.
You've questioned the stories you've carried.
You've made space for curiosity.
And maybe for the first time in a while, you've met yourself with compassion.

You've practiced noticing what's true.
You've remembered that not every thought deserves a seat at your table.
You've named the voices.
You've reclaimed your place at the head.

Remember, this isn't about perfection.
It's about presence.

Going forward, those old stories may still arise.
But now, you'll recognize them.
You'll breathe.
And you'll know—you get to choose which stories stay.

Because you are not your thoughts.
You are the one who sees, softens, and shifts them.

FIVE

What If You Weren't So Hard on Yourself?

Turning to Kindness as a Radical Act of Self-Love

"Talk to yourself like you would to someone you love."
— Brené Brown

At some point in the healing journey, the pain isn't just from what happened,
but from the story we told ourselves afterward,
how we continue to carry it,
and how we let it define us.

The inner voice whispering, *"I should be over this by now."*
The guilt that lingers, even after you've tried to make amends.
The shame that says, *"You should've known better."*

For many of us, especially those raised in the era of gold stars and self-sacrifice,
we were taught to equate achievement with worthiness.
We learned to strive, to hustle, to prove ourselves—again and again.

Somewhere along the way, we picked up the belief that being hard on ourselves
is how we grow, improve, and stay accountable.

But it didn't make us better, it just reinforced the message of unworthiness. It just made us tired.

Tired of never being enough.
Tired of holding it all together.
Tired of holding yourself to impossible standards, even in your pain.

Self-Compassion

We believed being hard on ourselves was how we stayed motivated, responsible, *"on track."* That if we gave ourselves too much grace, we'd lose our edge.

Yet here's the real truth.

Self-compassion isn't weakness; it's wisdom in action.
It's a superpower.
It's the birthplace of true transformation.

Psychologist Kristin Neff defines self-compassion as treating ourselves the way we'd treat a dear friend in a moment of struggle.

Simple. Radical. And for many of us, revolutionary.

It's made up of three essential elements—
Mindfulness: Noticing and being present with your pain, without minimizing or exaggerating it. Staying grounded without spiraling.
Common humanity: Remembering that struggle is part of being human. You're still learning; you're never alone.
Kindness: Offering yourself warmth, care, and understanding, especially when you fall short. Speaking to yourself like someone you love.

Here's what that looked like in my own life.

I didn't have a raging inner critic,
but I had an inner perfectionist.
The achiever. The fixer. The one who wanted to get it right and be the best and never be the one who dropped the ball.

When something went wrong, that voice would quietly ask,
"How did you miss that?"
"Why can't you just keep it together?"
"You're supposed to know better."

It didn't sound cruel. But it felt heavy.

And when I paused and asked, *"Would I say this to someone I love?"* The answer was no, not in a million years.
And when I started practicing self-compassion, I realized just how tired I was from trying to earn my own approval.

I pictured my younger self, tired, stretched too thin, doing her absolute best with what she had.
And I said to her what I needed to hear.

You're doing enough.
You're allowed to be tired. You're allowed to rest.
This is hard, and you're still good.
You don't have to prove your worth.
You are worthy already.

I wish I could say I believed it right away, but I didn't—not fully, not at first.

But I kept saying it.
Gently. Repeatedly.

Until my body began to soften.
Until my nervous system could breathe.
Until my inner critic got quieter, and I began to hear a different voice rising.
A kinder one.

This isn't about toxic positivity or empty affirmations.

This is about meeting yourself with a deeper truth and tenderness.

It's about choosing a voice that sees your effort, your heart, your healing, and says, with love, *"I'm here. You're okay. Keep going."*

✎ Pause & Ponder
Self-Compassion

Take a breath.
Let this land.

There's no rush. No performance. Just a space to be honest with kindness.

Here are a few gentle invitations.

Use what resonates. Leave the rest.

What's one area of your life in which you've been especially hard on yourself lately?

Write about it honestly. What story have you been telling yourself there?

What would it feel like to soften that voice just a little?

What might you say to yourself if you were someone you deeply loved?

Choose one that resonates:

1) Where did you first learn that being "strong" meant not needing anything?

What belief did that create, and is it still serving you?

2) Where did you learn that you had to be quiet, agreeable, or small to be safe?

What belief took root from that, and what might you reclaim now?

3) What was your earliest lesson about asking for help?

Was it welcomed, ignored, punished, or praised?

What kindness are you most needing right now?

Permission to rest? Grace for a mistake? Space to feel?

If you could write a compassionate letter to the version of yourself who's struggling, what would it say? Use this space to say what your heart has been longing to hear.

Loving-Kindness

Sometimes healing looks less like *striving*,
and more like *softening*.
Less like *doing* and more like *being*.

One of the most transformative practices I've found,
the kind that seeps in slowly and gently reshapes you from the inside out,
is the practice of loving-kindness.

In some traditions, it's called *metta* (Pali) or *maitri* (Sanskrit)—a quiet,
intentional well-wishing.
Not forced. Not performative. Just presence.

It's an invitation to open your heart to others... and, gently, to yourself.

The first time I tried it, I was sitting on a Florida beach.
The waves rolled in, steady and soft, a stark contrast to my inner storm.
I was carrying more than I ever had, and it was beginning to take its toll.
And someone in my life showed up, not with grand gestures, but with quiet,
steady love.
No fixing. Just holding space.

I found myself whispering silent blessings to them.
Then to myself.
Then, to the barista who'd handed me tea that morning.
Then, to someone I hadn't quite forgiven.
Then, to the world.

And I wept.

Not because anything had changed,
but because everything had softened.

This practice reminded me...
We can want good things for ourselves and others
without guilt, fear, or scarcity.
We can become vessels of love, even while we're still healing.

If you'd like to try it, here's how.
You can whisper the words, journal them, or simply hold them in your heart.
No pressure. No perfection. Just presence.

Sit comfortably.
Close your eyes, if that feels safe.
Place one hand over your heart.
Take a few slow breaths and settle into your body.

You can begin with yourself, or, if that feels too tender today, start with someone you love deeply.
Start where it feels easy. You can always widen the circle later.
This practice is yours. Let it meet you where you are.

If beginning with yourself:
Repeat the phrases three times—slowly, sincerely.

May I be safe.
May I be well.
May I be loved.
May I feel peace.

If starting with someone you love:
Bring them to mind, someone whose presence feels safe and true.
Send them the same blessings.

May you be safe.
May you be well.
May you be loved.
May you feel peace.

Then, if and when you're ready, gently bring that same loving-kindness back to yourself.

Now, bring to mind someone **neutral**.
Someone you don't know well—a grocery clerk, a neighbor you nod to, a face in passing.

Extend the same kindness to them.

May you be safe.
May you be well.
May you be loved.
May you feel peace.

Next, think of someone with whom you have a **challenge**.
You don't need to force forgiveness. Just open the door a crack.
Offer the blessings as best you can.

May you be safe.
May you be well.
May you be loved.
May you feel peace.

Finally, expand the circle to include **everyone, everywhere.**
Let the love ripple outward, to your friends, your neighbors, your community,
your country, and the world.

May all beings be safe.
May all beings be well.
May all beings be loved.
May all beings feel peace.

This isn't about pretending everything is fine.
It's about creating space where love can live.
It's about remembering that kindness,
offered inward and outward,
always matters.

Let this be your practice.
A quiet revolution of the heart.
A softening, not from weakness, but from wisdom.
Remembering that love—*especially for yourself*—has always been enough.

 Inspired Practice
Loving-Kindness

A quick guide to come back to anytime.

May I be safe.

May I be well.

May I be loved.

May I feel peace.

May you be safe.

May you be well.

May you be loved.

May you feel peace.

The traditional order:

1. A loved one
2. Yourself
3. A neutral person
4. A difficult person
5. All beings everywhere

✎ Pause & Ponder
Loving-Kindness

Take a deep breath and a soft pause.
You don't need to answer every question.
Just begin with the one that whispers to you.

What did it feel like to offer loving-kindness to yourself?
Was it easy? Tender? Unfamiliar?
What does that reveal about your relationship with yourself?

Who came to mind when you extended kindness outward?
Was it someone you love?
Someone who surprised you?
Someone you didn't expect?

What arose when you sent kindness to someone difficult?

What did you notice in your breath, your body, or your heart?

Which phrase felt the most alive to you?

Would you like to write your own? What words does your soul long to hear?

What would it feel like to begin your morning, or end your day, with this practice?

What version of you might emerge if kindness became your default setting?

Ho'oponopono

There's a practice with a name that may sound playful—Ho'oponopono—but its impact is anything but small.

Rooted in ancient Hawaiian tradition, *Ho'oponopono* loosely means *"to make right"* or *"to bring into balance."* Originally, it was a communal healing practice used among extended families to restore harmony and resolve conflict.

More recently, it gained global attention through the story of Dr. Ihaleakala Hew Len, a therapist at the Hawai'i State Hospital, who worked with criminally insane patients. Here's the remarkable part—he never met with them directly. As he sat with their case files, he silently practiced the four-line *Ho'oponopono* mantra:

"I'm sorry. Please forgive me. Thank you. I love you."

Over time, the energy of the hospital ward shifted—tension softened, incidents declined, and the atmosphere lightened. Not because the patients were *fixed*, but because they were being held differently. Seen differently.

It's an unusual story—perhaps even mythic at first glance.

But I've experienced the power of Ho'oponopono in my own life.

Years ago, I was carrying resentment toward an ex.
It wasn't always at the surface, but it was there.
It showed up in the background of my thoughts.
In the way I tensed during conversations.
In the quiet expectations I didn't even know I was still holding.

And if I'm being honest, a part of me clung to it.
Because forgiving felt too much like letting him off the hook.

But here's what I came to realize.
Holding on to resentment is like drinking poison
and hoping the other person suffers.

It's a weight that keeps you tethered to pain, long after the wound was created.

So I began whispering the four phrases.

Not to his face.
Not to manipulate.
Just for me. Just in prayer. Just in stillness.

I'm sorry.
Please forgive me.
Thank you.
I love you.

Not romantic love.
Not pretend-everything-is-okay love.
But a deeper kind of love.
The kind that whispers, *"I release you. I release me. I choose to let go."*

With practice, not perfection, I felt something loosen.

The anger didn't vanish overnight.
But it softened.
It stopped defining me.

And in its place, I found space.
Space for peace.
For surrender.
For softness.

Sometimes, healing isn't about figuring out the past.
It's about *clearing space* for what comes next.

☀〜 Inspired Practice
Ho'oponopono

A quick guide to come back to anytime.

I'm sorry.

Please forgive me.

Thank you.

I love you

✎ Pause & Ponder
Ho'oponopono

You don't have to be ready to forgive.
You don't have to force healing.
Just begin with honesty.

Let these reflections be an offering,
not to change the past, but to gently set yourself free.

Who or what have I been carrying, consciously or unconsciously?
What would it feel like to loosen my grip, even just a little?

Is there a relationship, memory, or moment that still echoes in my energy?
What might I be making space for if I chose to release it?

When I speak the four phrases,
I'm sorry. Please forgive me. Thank you. I love you.
How does my body respond? What part of me most needs to hear those words?

If I could speak to the younger version of me still holding the wound, what would I say?
Let this be a conversation, not a performance.

What would freedom feel like in this area of my life?
Let your nervous system answer. Let your breath respond.

You've softened.
You've witnessed yourself.
You've offered grace, both inward and outward.

This isn't the kind of work that comes with gold stars or tidy finish lines.
It's quieter than that, deeper than that.
And here's the truth
You're already changing.

Every time you choose love over judgment.
Every time you pause instead of reacting.
Every time you whisper,
"I see you. I forgive you. I'm learning to love you."
something shifts.

Let that be enough for now.

Because from this softer place, something new is already beginning to rise.
You've made space.
You've come home to yourself.

Now it's time to dream.

Next, we explore who you're becoming.
Not the roles you've played.
Not the masks you've worn.
But the truest version of you.
The one who's been waiting patiently to come through.

Scan the QR code to access the
Guided Meditations
or visit drdeonne.com/meditations

SIX

Change Your Story, Change Your Life

Softening Old Narratives and Reclaiming Your Voice

*"And the day came when the risk to remain tight in a bud
was more painful than the risk it took to blossom."*

— Anaïs Nin

There comes a moment, quiet but unmistakable, when we pause long enough
to ask,
"Is this the life I truly want?"

Not the one we were told to want.
Not the one that earns praise or fits neatly in a box.
But the one that feels like home in our own skin.

This is where the magic begins.
When we stop living by someone else's script and start writing our own.
When we surrender the story of who we *should* be and remember who we *are*.

Not because we've failed or broken.
But because our soul is ready for more.

More freedom.
More truth.
More love.

And here's what's wild and wonderful...
When we begin to love ourselves—truly, wholly—our capacity to love others expands beyond anything we imagined.

Rewriting your story isn't about denying the past.
It's about reclaiming your pen.
Choosing what to carry forward and what to lovingly leave behind.

This chapter is your invitation to become the author of what's next.
With clarity. With courage. With compassion.

To-Be List

I remember an experience that cracked my heart wide open and shifted my lens on life, permanently.

It was December 2012. I was headed to Guatemala on a humanitarian expedition, carrying far more than just gear. Tucked inside my suitcase were weariness, heartache, and a hope so faint I almost missed it. I thought I was going to help others. I didn't realize how much the journey would heal me too.

Somewhere along that trip, I picked up a book that suggested a simple practice—*make a list of what you want in a future partner.*

At first, it felt light. Almost playful.
And I followed the nudge. I opened a fresh page and began to write.

After the relationships I'd been through, I was ready to get clear.

So I started dreaming.
Kindness.
Emotional intelligence.
Adventure.

Spiritual curiosity.
Laughter. Partnership. Safety. A co-creator. A best friend.

The list grew, eventually including more than 70 qualities.

And then, like so many dreams we quietly dare to name, I tucked it away and forgot about it.

Almost a decade later, I stumbled across it again. I was in a serious relationship at the time, and I showed the list to the man I was dating. I was proud. Lit up. Grateful that I had brought someone like him into my life.

He read it, looked up, and said:

"You know you're all of this, right?"

And something shifted.

Because I realized the list wasn't about him.
It was never really a wish list.
It was always a *To-Be list*.

A reflection of the woman I was becoming.
Kind. Creative. Curious. Emotionally intelligent. Strong. Playful. Present.
And yes, **adventurous**. *(No surprise there, right?)*

All the things I once thought I needed to find in someone else were already within me.
They just needed space and permission to rise.

Not long after, I shared the list with my dad.
I was proud of who I was becoming—of the clarity, the growth, the woman I'd worked so hard to become.
And if I'm honest, I was still hoping he'd see it too.

But instead of celebration, I was met with something else.

I don't remember his exact words, but the energy was clear, *"Who do you think you are to dream that big?"*

It stung.
And at the time, it hurt more than I wanted it to.
I was still looking for his approval. Hoping, deep down, he'd recognize what I had grown into.

But now I see, he wasn't talking to me.
He was speaking from the limits he'd accepted for his own life.

Dreaming big scared him.
And watching me do it, without apology?
That made him uncomfortable.

But I'm not here to play small, to keep others comfortable.
And neither are you.

The truth is, rewriting your story begins with giving yourself *permission to dream again.*
To imagine what's possible.
To notice where you've been settling, not because you wanted to, but because you didn't yet believe more was available.

This is where you begin to write a new story.

Not from fantasy. Not from pressure.
But from the quiet knowing that who you are, *and who you're becoming*, is worth it.

You've done the work to soften.
To listen inward.
To tend to your heart, your mind, your stories.

Now you're ready to go deeper.
To shine a light on the beliefs that have been shaping your life, often quietly, in the background.

☀︎〰︎ Inspired Practice
Create Your To-Be List

This isn't a list of things to achieve.
It's a reflection of who you're becoming,
the woman aligned with her truth, not someone else's expectations.

Imagine the kind of partner, friend, leader, or future you want to call in.
What qualities light you up? What energy do you want to be surrounded by?

Then shift inward.
How can I embody the very energy I've been seeking?

Make your list.
Not of what to do, but who to be.

Let it reflect your values, your vision, your voice.
Let it surprise you.

And when you're ready—own it.

Because you are allowed to take up space.
To live fully.
To become everything you were always meant to be.

Use the following two pages to begin your To-Be List.
Let it rise from your heart, not your to-do list.
Write freely. Dream bravely. Surprise yourself.

And if it feels more natural to create a digital version—a note on your phone, a private document—*that's beautiful, too.*

What matters most is that it lives somewhere you'll return to.
Somewhere it can grow with you.

This isn't just a list.
It's a mirror. A map. A manifesto.

And it begins here.

Name It to Tame It

This next section invites you to do something both radical and gentle.
To name the old story—and choose a new one.
It's simple, but powerful.

Because the stories we carry shape the choices we make.
And when we change the narrative, we begin to shape the future.

Each set of pages that follows explores a different area of life, categories you may recognize from the Bloomprint in Chapter 1.

On the left, you'll find examples of common beliefs many of us have carried. Some will feel familiar. Some may stir something deeper.

On the right, you'll find a blank page to explore your own.

☀〰 Inspired Practice
Name It to Tame It

Start with just one area of your life.
You don't have to have it all figured out.
You just have to begin.

Write the old belief in *pencil*—lightly, honestly.
It's not permanent. It's not final.
It's just something you believed... until now.

Then, underneath it, in **pen** (blue, purple, or whatever color makes you smile),
write the new story you're choosing instead.

For example:
Old belief (in pencil): "I have to hold it all together or everything will fall apart."
New belief (in pen): "It's safe to let go. I don't have to do it all."

You don't have to believe the new story 100%—yet.
Just be willing to try it on.

This is the beginning of your rewrite.
Because small shifts?
They open big doors.

Work & Contribution

Let's begin here. Not because you need to have it all figured out, but because this is often where we've tied our worth to our output.

Work and contribution can carry a quiet weight.
Many of us were taught to measure success by productivity, performance, and pushing through.
We became masters of multitasking, climbing, proving, and doing.

But somewhere along the way, we may have lost the joy.
Or the meaning.
Or the part of us that dreamed in the first place.

It's okay if this part of your life feels heavy, or complicated, or uncertain.
This isn't about starting over.
It's about telling the truth.

What have you believed about work, success, ambition, or your own capability?
What stories were handed to you from parents, teachers, or culture?
And what story would you like to live instead?

Here are a few old narratives that may sound familiar:

    ✗ *Success means sacrificing myself.*
    ✗ *I'm too old to start something new.*
    ✗ *I have to stay. I'm lucky to have this job.*

Now imagine flipping just one of those stories:

    ➤ **Success means honoring my energy and doing work that feels meaningful to me.**

That small shift? It's enough to begin again.

Write your old story in pencil—you can always erase it. Then, in pen, write the story you're ready to practice believing.

Home & Surroundings

Let's bring awareness to the spaces that surround you.
Your home. Your workspace. Your car.
The rooms you move through each day.

These spaces are not neutral.
They shape your energy, clarity, and ability to exhale.

For many women, especially those who carry a lot for others,
the environment becomes a reflection of what we're holding inside.

The things we keep *"just in case."*
The piles we'll sort through *"when there's time."*
The decor that no longer feels like us.

This isn't about perfection. It's about resonance.

Does your space reflect who you are, who you've been, or who you want to become?

Is it working *with* you or against the life you want to create?
Here are a few old narratives that may sound familiar:

✗ *It's selfish to create a space that's just for me.*
✗ *I can't change anything until I move or renovate.*
✗ *This space reflects my chaos, and I don't even know where to start.*

Now imagine flipping just one of those stories:

➤ **I'm allowed to create beauty and peace in my space, one corner at a time.**

You don't have to overhaul everything.
You just get to begin, where you are, with what you have.

Let one slight shift create room for more of what you truly want.

Write your old story in pencil—you can always erase it. Then, in pen, write the story you're ready to practice believing.

Money & Finances

This one can stir up a lot of feelings
because money isn't just about numbers.

It's about worth. Safety. Security. Foundation.

And for many of us, it's tangled up with stories we didn't even know we inherited.

We absorbed beliefs from our families, our cultures, our early experiences.
We noticed how people around us talked (or *didn't* talk) about money.
We learned what was "too much," what was "not enough," and where we were supposed to land in between.

But what if those stories aren't yours to carry anymore?

What if money didn't have to be a source of stress or shame?
What if it could become a tool for alignment, expansion, and generosity?
What if money simply magnifies the goodness already within you?

Here are a few old narratives that may sound familiar:

- ✗ *I'm just not good with money.*
- ✗ *Wanting more makes me greedy.*
- ✗ *I'll never be able to get ahead.*

Now imagine flipping just one of those stories:

➤ **I'm learning to steward my money with clarity and confidence.**

You don't need to have it all figured out.
You just get to begin rewriting your relationship with money,
one belief, one budget, one brave decision at a time.

Let it be less about control...
and more about conscious care.

Write your old story in pencil—you can always erase it. Then, in pen, write the story you're ready to practice believing.

Physical Vitality

Your body is one of your greatest gifts.
It's where your stories live.
It's how you move through the world.
It holds the joy, the grief, the growth,
and the wisdom of every season you've lived.

And yet, many of us have spent years,
sometimes decades, disconnected from our bodies.

We've learned to criticize.
To compare.
To push through.

We were taught to shrink.
To ignore pain.
To override intuition.
To wait until things got bad enough to change.

But your body doesn't need to be fixed.
You get to honor it now, exactly as you are.

Here are a few old narratives that may sound familiar:

   ✗ *I don't belong at the gym.*
   ✗ *I'm too old to start now.*
   ✗ *I just don't have time to take care of myself.*

Now imagine flipping just one of those stories:

   ➤ **My body is worthy of care, strength, and gentleness—at every age and every stage.**

You don't have to do it perfectly.
You just get to begin.

By listening inward.
By moving with love.
By treating your body like a beloved companion, because she is.

Write your old story in pencil—you can always erase it. Then, in pen, write the story you're ready to practice believing.

Creativity & Play

Play isn't frivolous.
It's not something you earn after the real work is done.

It's how you reconnect with your joy.
It's where your creativity comes alive.
And it's often one of the first things to disappear when life gets busy, heavy, or overwhelming.

Many of us were raised to value productivity.
To measure our days by outputs and accomplishments.

But you weren't born to be a machine.
You were born to feel.
To create.
To laugh.
To play.

Reclaiming joy is part of healing.
Reclaiming fun is part of coming home to yourself.

Here are a few old narratives that may sound familiar:

   ✗ *I don't have time for play.*
   ✗ *It's selfish to do things just for me.*
   ✗ *I'm not creative.*

Now imagine flipping just one of those stories:

   ➤ **Joy is essential, not optional, and I deserve to make space for it.**

Fun isn't a detour.
It's the slingshot that draws you inward,
just long enough to launch you forward
with joy, energy, and ease.

Write your old story in pencil—you can always erase it. Then, in pen, write the story you're ready to practice believing.

Emotional Well-Being

Emotional well-being doesn't always announce itself.
Sometimes it's tucked behind a tight smile.
Sometimes it hides in the pushing through, the holding it together, the quiet "I'm fine."

We're often taught to override our feelings in the name of strength—
to stay busy, push through, hold it all together, and never ask for help.

But when we numb the hard feelings,
we dull the joyful ones too.

Struggling doesn't make you weak.
Asking for support doesn't make you a burden.
You don't have to handle everything on your own.

Tuning in isn't a weakness; it's wisdom.
And caring for your emotional world doesn't mean something's wrong.
It simply means you're human.

Here are a few old narratives that may sound familiar:

    ✗ *I should be able to handle this by myself.*
    ✗ *If I don't do it, no one else will.*
    ✗ *If I slow down, it will all fall apart.*

Now imagine flipping just one of those stories:

    ➤ **I'm allowed to rest, ask for help, and let go of things that were never mine to carry.**

Tending to your inner world
is not selfish,
it's sacred.

Write your old story in pencil—you can always erase it. Then, in pen, write the story you're ready to practice believing.

Friends

Friendship in adulthood can be beautiful
and complicated.

Some friendships grow with us.
Some drift quietly away.
Some stay in our lives out of habit, guilt, or history.
And some leave a lasting mark, even if they don't last.

As we evolve, our connections often shift.
But many of us were taught to keep showing up,
even when the relationship no longer feels aligned.

We don't want to hurt anyone.
We worry about being too much.
Or not enough.

But friendship isn't about obligation.
It's about safety. Reciprocity. Joy.

You're allowed to outgrow relationships.
And you're allowed to nurture the ones worth keeping—
to speak honestly,
to show up with love,
and to be seen as you truly are.

Here are a few old narratives that may sound familiar:

✗ *I have to stay close to people I've known forever.*
✗ *If I don't initiate, the friendship will fade.*
✗ *I shouldn't need new friends at this age.*

Now imagine flipping just one of those stories:

➤ **I'm allowed to build friendships that reflect who I am now, not just who I used to be.**

Write your old story in pencil—you can always erase it. Then, in pen, write the story you're ready to practice believing.

Romantic Connection

Romantic relationships can be some of our most profound teachers.
They often reveal where we feel secure,
and where we still carry fear.

They invite us to open, to grow,
to be seen more fully than almost anywhere else.
Many of us learned to care deeply, sometimes at the expense of ourselves.
We learned to accommodate. To stay. To try harder.

But love doesn't have to mean losing yourself.
It can be where you come home.

Whether you're single, partnered, questioning, healing, or redefining what love
means—this space is for you.

What do you long for?
What are you learning about giving and receiving love?
What would it look like to be fully met—
by yourself first, and then, maybe, by another?

Relationships are a mirror.
Not to show you what's wrong,
but to reflect the parts of you still asking for love.

And at the root of it all is this truth...
You are the one you've been waiting for.

Here are a few old narratives that may sound familiar:

- ✗ *If I love them enough, they'll change.*
- ✗ *Maybe I'm too much or not enough.*
- ✗ *I just need to be less needy.*

Now imagine flipping just one of those stories:

- ➤ **I deserve a relationship where I feel safe, seen, and supported, and that starts with me.**

Write your old story in pencil—you can always erase it. Then, in pen, write the story you're ready to practice believing.

Family

Family is often where our first stories are written—
about love, safety, worth.

Who we're supposed to be.
How much space we're allowed to take up.
What's okay to feel, and what isn't.

These stories can run deep.
Even if we've created distance,
set boundaries,
or built a chosen family,
those early messages can still echo.

This isn't about blame.
It's about awareness.

You get to hold compassion for your past,
and choose something different in the present.

To acknowledge what was handed down,
and decide what continues.

You get to rewrite the story,
one truth at a time.

Here are a few old narratives that may sound familiar:

   ✗ *I'm responsible for keeping the peace.*
   ✗ *It's easier to stay quiet than to start a fight.*
   ✗ *I have to earn love by being good.*

Now imagine flipping just one of those stories:

   ➤ **I can love my family, born or chosen, and still honor my truth, my boundaries, and my needs.**

Write your old story in pencil—you can always erase it. Then, in pen, write the story you're ready to practice believing.

Personal Growth

Somewhere along the way, you realized—
This can't be all there is.

Maybe it was a quiet discontent.
A restless stirring.
A nudge from your soul whispering,
There's more.

Personal growth doesn't always start with a vision.
Sometimes, it begins with a breakdown.
A burnout.
A holy unraveling.

And from that place,
something sacred begins to form.

You don't need to be fixed.
You are not a project.
You are a person, remembering your own power.

Growth isn't about becoming someone else.
It's about becoming more of who you really are.

Here are a few old narratives that may sound familiar:

- ✗ *I'll start when I have more time.*
- ✗ *I should be further along by now.*
- ✗ *Maybe this is just how I am.*

Now imagine flipping just one of those stories:

➤ **Growth is happening, even when it's quiet. I trust the pace that's right for me.**

Write your old story in pencil—you can always erase it. Then, in pen, write the story you're ready to practice believing.

Spirituality

Spirituality isn't always found in a sanctuary.
Sometimes it's in the stillness before sunrise.
In the moonlight resting on mountain peaks.
In the sound of waves meeting the shore.
In the hush of a river winding past your feet.

It's the sense that something greater is holding you,
even when everything else feels uncertain.

This isn't about religion.
It's about connection.

To yourself.
To something bigger.
To the mystery that can't always be named or explained.

You don't need a specific path to be spiritual.
You don't need to get it "right."
You just have to listen for the quiet within,
the part that remembers *you are already whole.*

Whether you're rediscovering your faith, releasing old beliefs,
or finding a new way forward,
your spiritual journey gets to be uniquely yours.

Here are a few old narratives that may sound familiar:

✗ *I'm not spiritual enough to hear my intuition.*
✗ *I need to earn peace by doing more.*
✗ *If I'm struggling, it must mean I'm doing something wrong.*

Now imagine flipping just one of those stories:

➤ **I am already connected. My soul knows the way, even when I don't have all the answers.**

Write your old story in pencil—you can always erase it. Then, in pen, write the story you're ready to practice believing.

Legacy & Impact

You are here for a reason.
Not to fix everything. Not to save everyone.
But to offer something only you can give.

Your contribution doesn't have to be loud.
It doesn't have to go viral.
It might be how you show up,
in your family, your workplace, your community.

It might be the way you listen.
The way you create.
The way you lead with heart.

You don't have to burn out to make a difference.
And you don't have to have it all figured out to begin.

Sometimes legacy is the way you use your voice.
Sometimes impact is found in choosing rest so others know they can, too.
Sometimes it's simply being who you are,
fully, unapologetically, and with love.

Here are a few old narratives that may sound familiar:

✗ *I need to do something big to matter.*
✗ *Other people are already doing it better.*
✗ *I don't know enough to make a difference.*

Now imagine flipping just one of those stories:

➤ **I'm already making a difference, just by living with intention and love.**

And that? That's more than enough.

Write your old story in pencil—you can always erase it. Then, in pen, write the story you're ready to practice believing.

✎ Pause & Ponder
Name It to Tame It

You just did something rare.
You paused.
You looked inward.
You told the truth.

Take a moment to notice what that felt like.
— *Which stories were most challenging to name? Which surprised you?*
— *Where did you feel resistance? Where did you feel release?*
— *What new truths are ready to shape your next chapter?*

Let these answers rise gently.
You're not just rewriting stories.
You're rewriting what's possible.

Let this page hold the truths that are still finding their way to you.

You've done something most people never pause long enough to do.

You've named the stories that no longer serve you.
You've honored where they came from, without shame or blame.
And you've begun the sacred work of choosing new ones.

Each belief you rewrote was more than a mindset shift;
it was a declaration.
A quiet reclaiming.
A return to the truth of who you are and what you deserve.

This chapter brought your Bloomprint into focus,
not just as a reflection of your now,
but as a map for your becoming.

And now, with this new clarity, you're ready for the next step—
not to "fix" your life,
but to design it with intention and heart.

In the next chapter, we'll explore what it looks like to dream on purpose,
to shape a vision that feels aligned, expansive, and deeply personal.

We'll look at tools that support that dream,
vision boards, audio affirmations, and a more soulful approach to setting
intentions.

Because transformation isn't just about what you release.
It's about what you're ready to create next.

SEVEN

Dream Bigger, Live Braver

Giving Yourself Permission to Want More, Without Apology

"Tell me, what is it you plan to do with your one wild and precious life?"
— Mary Oliver

You've done sacred work to get here.
You've told the truth about where you are.
You've softened, released, and remembered who you really are.
You've released the beliefs that no longer fit and reclaimed the ones that do.

Now, you get to dream.

Not the kind of dreaming that feels like escape,
but the kind that roots you deeper into possibility.
The kind that whispers, *"What if this is only the beginning?"*

This chapter is not about pressure.
It's about design.
It's not about perfection.
It's about permission.

You won't be mapping out a five-year plan.

You'll be tuning into the quiet, steady pulse of your becoming and asking, *"What do I want life to feel like from here forward?"*

You'll move through a series of soulful tools to help you clarify and create:

- A Dream Life Grid to map your values and desires
- A Vision Board to give your dreams texture and shape
- A Dream Life Audio to bring it all to life through your own voice

This is not about hustle.

It's about alignment.

It's about imagining a life that reflects who you truly are and giving yourself permission to begin living it, now.

Dream Life Grid

You've rewritten the old stories.

Now it's time to imagine how life might feel when it reflects your values, your truth, and your vision.

This grid is a starting point, not for chasing an ideal, but for envisioning possibilities.

What would *wholeness* or *deep alignment* feel like in each area of your life? Write a word. Sketch a symbol. Doodle your dreams.

There's no right way, only *your* way.

What does *fulfillment* look like in each of these areas? What does *peace* look like? *Joy? Alignment?*

Let this be a brainstorm for the masterpiece to come, your **Vision Board.**

And know this—

You can come back to this anytime.

As you grow, your dreams will, too.

This is not a one-and-done moment.

This is a living invitation to keep imagining, evolving, and becoming.

☀︎〰 Inspired Practice
Dream Life Grid

In each square, name what alignment looks or feels like for you.

You can write a word, a feeling, or a complete sentence.
You can draw a symbol, color in a square, or leave space open for what's still unfolding.

You're not crafting a final draft.
You're planting seeds of possibility.
Let them settle. Let them speak.
Let them take root.

Personal Growth	Spirituality	Legacy & Impact
Family	Romantic Connection	Friends
Physical Vitality	Creativity & Play	Emotional Well-Being
Work & Contribution	Home & Surroundings	Money & Finances

Vision Board

A vision board isn't just a creative exercise.
It's a declaration.

It's you saying:
This is what I want.
This is what I'm ready for.
This is who I'm becoming.

And the best part?
It doesn't have to be fancy or flawless.
It just has to feel like *you*.

After completing your Dream Life Grid, this is your invitation to shape your dreams into something you can see and believe in.

Some women gather magazines and scissors. Others, like me, curate images online and arrange them in Canva or on Google Slides. You might love Pinterest. You might prefer both, a physical board in your bedroom *and* a digital version as your phone's lock screen.

Remember, there's no right way, just *your* way.

Some dreams feel big. That's okay.
One strategy I love is *layering*.

Let's say you're working toward saving $10,000.
Start with a $1,000 milestone, then layer the next underneath—using whatever increments and milestones make sense to you. Maybe it looks like this:
$1,000
$2,000
$5,000
And at the bottom? $10,000 saved.

Each time you reach a new milestone, peel off the top layer.
Celebrate it. Feel the momentum building.
Let yourself see and savor the progress.

☀︎〰 Inspired Practice
Vision Board

Create a vision board that speaks to your future.
Not just what you want to have, but how you want to *feel*.

Choose images, colors, and textures that stir something in your soul.
Layer in your values. Let it be playful. Let it be bold. Let it be you.

This isn't about chasing someone else's idea of a perfect life.
It's about coming home to what resonates within you.

When a vision becomes real, move it to your **Celebration Journal** and mark the moment.
Let it be your proof to know deeply:
Your energy is powerful.
Your dreams are valid.
And the life you're creating is already unfolding.

☀︎〜 Inspired Practice
Celebration Journal

Your Celebration Journal is a sacred space to acknowledge and honor your inner and outer achievements, both big and small.

Tape in the image. Add a date.
Write a few words about how it happened, how it felt, or what it meant to you.

This isn't just a scrapbook of wins.
It's a mirror of your growth.

Return often.
Celebrate often.
This is your proof of becoming.

Celebration Journal
This is where you honor the becoming.
Tape your image here. Add a note, a feeling, a date.
Let it remind you.
You are the kind of woman who makes dreams real.

Celebration Journal

Take a moment. Mark the win.

Everything counts.

Your dreams are unfolding because of you.

Celebration Journal

Another dream, made real.

Celebrate. Reflect. Trust.

You're becoming her; the woman you are.

Dream Life Audio

You've shaped your vision with clarity and intention.
Now, it's time to give it a voice.

A Dream Life Audio is exactly what it sounds like—your dream, spoken aloud
and recorded so you can listen again and again.

The repetition isn't just a feel-good ritual.
It rewires your subconscious.
It anchors you in who you're becoming.

I discovered this practice years ago, and I've loved seeing it take off through
social media, especially now that AI can help bring your vision to life.
Think of it as a creative partner here to serve your clarity, not complicate it.

☀︎〰 Inspired Practice
Dream Life Audio

Start with your Dream Life Grid.
Reflect on each area of your life.

How do you want to feel?
What do you want to experience, embody, create?

Now write.
Use your own words.
Keep it real.
Keep it *you*.

Your subconscious believes what sounds like your voice,
so let it be personal.

Infuse it with emotion.
Instead of just saying, *"I am healthy,"* try,
"I feel energized, vibrant, and alive in my body."

Be specific. Be sensory. Let it come alive.

Then choose music that speaks to your soul.
Gentle piano. Meditation tracks. Bold cinematic scores.
There's no wrong choice. Let it move you.

Now record. Keep it simple.
Play your music from one device and record using your phone's recording app.
No fancy gear required, just presence and permission.

A tip? Keep it under five minutes so you'll actually listen.

Find a quiet space where you feel grounded and safe.
This is sacred work.

Let it be simple.
Let it be powerful.
Let it be yours.

How do you want to feel? Don't overthink or edit—just let the words flow.

Write down how you most want to feel in your dream life. Use single words, short phrases, even fragments.

Joyful. Free. Grounded. Energized. Connected. Radiant.

Capture whatever rises up. This is the raw material you'll shape into the script for your Dream Life Audio on the next few pages.

This is the space to draft the script for your Dream Life Audio. Take the words you captured on the previous page and begin shaping them into a script.

Write as if it's happening right now—in the present tense, as though you're already living it. Let it flow.

You might start with simple statements like:

- I am...
- I feel...
- I experience...
- I am surrounded by...

Use as much detail and emotion as you can. This isn't about outside perfection, it's about creating a vision that excites you and pulls you forward, even if it doesn't feel real yet.

Let your heart lead the way.

Gentle—Ideal—Stretch

You've dared to dream.
You've created a vision you can see, hear, and feel.

Now, let's talk about what brings that dream to life—*aligned action.*

This isn't about hustle or pressure or rigid timelines.
Not every step needs to be huge.
In fact, the most sustainable changes often start *small,*
anchored in kind intention, shaped by natural rhythms,
and aligned with your energy.

That's why I love the Gentle—Ideal—Stretch approach.

It's flexible.
It's empowering.
And it meets you *exactly where you are.*

Let's replace pressure with possibility.

- **Gentle Goal:** The bare-minimum, no-shame version. Even on your hardest week, you could do this.
- **Ideal Goal:** The sweet spot. Feels doable, energizing, and aligned with your dream life.
- **Stretch Goal:** The bold version. You won't hit it every week, and you don't need to. But when you do? You'll feel powerful.

Let's say you want to care for your body more deeply.
No more extremes. No more punishment. Just presence and reverence. You might begin here.

- **Gentle:** Three times a week for 15 minutes of movement: stretching, walking, dancing in the kitchen.
- **Ideal:** Move your body four times a week for 30 minutes.
- **Stretch:** Five times a week for an hour, whatever feels expansive and aligned.

Or maybe you're longing to feel more connected, whether that's in your friendships, your partnership, or yourself. Try this rhythm.

- **Gentle:** Reach out with something simple— a quick text, voice note, or an invitation to walk and talk.
- **Ideal:** One meaningful moment of connection each week. *(One of my favorite practices is a weekly date with myself. No explanation needed. Just permission.)*
- **Stretch:** A weekend away, a sister circle, or time carved out just for you.

Perhaps you're feeling the nudge for growth—not the kind that overwhelms, but the kind that *quietly excites you.* Consider one of these ideas.

- **Gentle:** A small habit shift every few months.
- **Ideal:** One meaningful experience a year, something that stretches you gently—a retreat, a trip, a new skill.
- **Stretch**: Saying yes to the wild idea that's been *tugging at your soul.*

None of this is about doing it perfectly.
It's about *moving with intention.*

☀〰 Inspired Practice
Gentle—Ideal—Stretch

Choose one area of your life that's asking for your attention.
It could be your body, your creativity, your relationships, your space—anything stirring within you.

Then ask yourself:

- What's my **Gentle** goal?
  The minimum that still feels meaningful. A tender promise to keep showing up for you.
- What's my **Ideal** goal?
  The rhythm that feels energizing and aligned with your dream life.
- What's my **Stretch** goal?
  The bold version. A little outside your comfort zone. A lot closer to your becoming.

Write them down.
Let them breathe. Let them flex. Let them evolve.

Remember, this isn't about perfection.
It's about showing up with intention.

Week by week.
Step by step.
You're living it.

Choose one area of your life that feels ready for attention—your body, your relationships, or your growth—and reflect on your gentle, ideal, and stretch goals. What feels aligned right now? What would feel exciting to grow into?

Gentle: A small, manageable step that feels easy and kind
Ideal: Your realistic, grounded intention—the one that fits your life now
Stretch: Your bold, future-you version—the one that calls you forward

This framework is one you can return to again and again.
Apply it to any area of your Bloomprint—your body, your creativity, your relationships, your space—anywhere growth is calling you.

Gentle: A small, manageable step that feels easy and kind
Ideal: A realistic intention that fits your life now
Stretch: A bold, future-you version that expands your comfort zone.

Looking across the goals you've named, what do you notice? Where do you feel most called to take action? What fears or resistance showed up, and how might you meet those gently?

✎ Pause & Ponder
Becoming Her

You've dreamed with intention.
You've named what alignment looks like.
You've given your future a voice, a face, and a path forward.

Now... take a breath.

Let your body catch up to the vision in your heart and mind.
Let your nervous system feel the safety of expansion.

And ask yourself:
— *What feels most alive in my dream life right now?*
— *What energy do I want to embody this week?*
— *What does the future me want me to know today?*

Let these answers rise softly.

This isn't a finish line.
It's a threshold.
You're not just dreaming—you're becoming.

You've done more than dream—you've **declared**.

With your **Dream Life Grid**, you gave form to your desires.
With your **Vision Board**, you gave them a face.
With your **Dream Life Audio**, you gave them a voice.
And with your **Gentle—Ideal—Stretch goals**, you gave them traction.

This is the work of becoming,
not just imagining who you could be,
but choosing, day by day, to live in alignment with her.

To act.
To celebrate progress.
To move forward, even if the steps are small.

You're no longer waiting for permission.
You're no longer waiting for perfect conditions.
You're *doing* it. You're *living* it.

And now, it's time to take a closer look at what surrounds you—
Your energy.
Your space.
Your habits.
Your people.

Because becoming isn't just about what you say yes to—
it's about what you're no longer willing to let in.

Scan the QR code to access
your **Dream Life Grid**
or visit drdeonne.com/dream

EIGHT

Watch What You Feed

Curating the Inputs That Shape Your Energy, Focus, and Life

"You are the gatekeeper of your own life.
Choose wisely what you allow through the door."

— Oprah Winfrey

A grandmother once told her granddaughter,
"Inside each of us are two wolves.
One is full of anger, fear, jealousy, and blame.
The other is full of love, peace, generosity, and truth."

The girl asked, *"Which wolf wins?"*
The grandmother replied, *"The one you feed."*

Maybe you've been feeling overwhelmed lately, stretched thin by the noise, the clutter, the constant pull of too much. You're not alone. When life gets loud, we often default to feeding the fear. The doubt. The overgiving. The distraction.

But what if the shift begins not with a big leap, but with a small, subtle noticing?

This chapter isn't just about decluttering your home or setting boundaries.
It's about awareness.
It's about noticing what you let in—what you watch, scroll, or believe—because every click, bite, or thought feeds the story you're living.

Because everything you take in?
Feeds something.

Your thoughts.
Your habits.
Your energy.
Your inner peace.

They're all shaped by what you choose to nourish.

Peace isn't always something you earn.
Sometimes, it's something you protect by being fiercely intentional with your inputs.

We often think of *diet* as what we eat.
But your whole diet is everything you consume.

The shows you binge.
The voices you follow.
The commitments you say yes to.
The behaviors you tolerate.
What you whisper to yourself when no one else is listening.

The question isn't, *"Am I consuming too much?"*
It's, *"What am I feeding and what's growing in me because of it?"*

This chapter is an invitation to pause.
To look gently within and ask,
"Does this nourish the life I'm creating?"
"Does this align with the woman I'm becoming?"

Is your home a source of *quiet chaos*—or a *sanctuary* that supports you?
Are you running on *autopilot*—or moving with *intention*?
Are your digital inputs feeding your *doubt*—or fueling your *light*?

You don't need to overhaul everything overnight.
But awareness creates choices.
And small, intentional shifts?
They can change everything.

Shape Your Space with Intention

You can't always control what happens outside your door.
But what lives inside your home, your car, your closet, your fridge, that's yours
to curate.

Your environment is more than décor.
It's the *energetic soil* where your well-being is rooted.
It whispers to your nervous system all day long,
"You're safe here.
Or you're not."

So let's pause and listen.

What story is your space telling right now?
Does it soothe you or stimulate you? Is it filled with intention or with things
you no longer need, love, or even notice?

As you already know, this isn't about perfection.
It's about *alignment*.

Are your surroundings making it easier to become who you're becoming...
or are they quietly keeping you tied to an older version of yourself?

Maybe it's a pantry filled with foods that drain you.
Maybe it's a nightstand cluttered with unread books and undone to-do lists.
Maybe it's a car that feels more like a mobile junk drawer than a space for peace.

We've all been there.

But here's the beautiful truth.
You can shift the energy by shifting anything, even one drawer.
One shelf. One room. One ritual.

Decluttering isn't just about tidying up.
It's also about creating space—for energy, creativity, clarity, and calm.
It's about creating harmony between your outer space and your inner state.

What if you thought of your home as a sacred partner in your transformation?
What if it could rise to meet you?

Start small.
Start true.
What space is asking to be reset?

✎ Pause & Ponder
Tend Your Sacred Soil

— *Which areas of your space reflect who you are becoming and which ones reflect who you used to be?*
— *What have you outgrown that still takes up space in your home... or your heart?*
— *Where in your home do you feel most at ease? How might you create more?*

Choose Who Has Access to Your Energy

If your home is your foundation,
your relationships are your *frequency*.
They shape your days, influence your thoughts,
and either nourish or drain your energy.

This isn't about blame.
It's about awareness.

Who do you let close?
Who gets your energy, your time, your trust?

Some people light you up.
Others dim your glow.
Some relationships are rooted in love but tangled in obligation.
Others feel like sunlight, warm, effortless, and true.

We've been taught to keep showing up,
to stay loyal no matter the cost.

But what if the cost is your peace?
Your purpose?
Your presence?

You become the average of the people you spend the most time with.
So choose wisely.
Lovingly.
Intentionally.

Let this be a season of *gentle discernment.*

Not every text deserves a reply.
Not every invitation is meant for you.
Not every connection is meant to last forever.

You're allowed to shift.
To step back.
To set down what you've been carrying.

To choose *reciprocity over resentment.*
To let people be who they are
and still choose what's best for you.

This is about *alignment*, not abandonment.
It's about making room for the people who meet you
with curiosity, kindness, and care.

Your heart knows.
And you don't need to justify your clarity.

✎ Pause & Ponder
Discern with Love

— *Who feels like sunlight in your life, warm, nourishing, real?*
— *Are there relationships you've outgrown, but haven't released?*
— *Where are you overextending and what boundaries might restore balance?*

Clear the Feed

Your mind is where your stories live.
Your thoughts, your focus, your attention,
they shape your experience of the world.

And in today's world, your thoughts are being constantly influenced by what surrounds you.

This is your invitation to become more intentional with what you let in.
What are you consuming daily, on your phone, in your earbuds, on your screen?
What news, noise, or narratives are shaping your beliefs?
Which voices feel empowering and which ones leave you feeling anxious, inadequate, or overwhelmed?

Sometimes, we follow people we don't even like.
We scroll past content that slowly wears down our confidence.
We let algorithms decide what fills our minds and what lingers in our hearts.

But you get to *reclaim* that power.

Curate your inputs the way you'd curate a sacred space,
with care, with discernment, with intention.

Unfollow accounts that drain you.
Unsubscribe from the noise.
Mute the chaos long enough to hear your own thoughts again.

And then, fill that space with something more aligned. Or simply allow a bit more silence and quiet into your life. You chose.

Follow thought leaders who *inspire* you.
Choose books, podcasts, and playlists that *light* you up.
Replace comparison with *curiosity*.
Replace criticism with *compassion*.
Replace consuming with *creating*.

You're not just protecting your peace.
You're reshaping your reality, one input at a time.

✎ Pause & Ponder
Feed What Feeds You

— *Which inputs leave you feeling expanded, and which leave you feeling empty?*
— *If your thoughts echoed your digital diet, what message would they be repeating?*
— *Where might you be craving stillness? Curiosity? Truth?*

You've explored what surrounds you
and the quiet landscapes within.

You've brought awareness to patterns, people, and spaces shaping your days.
You've paused to notice what nourishes you and what no longer does.

Now, it's time to listen.
Not to the noise of the world,
but to the quiet wisdom that's already inside you.

The questions that follow aren't here to grade or judge.
They're here to guide.
To invite.
To meet you exactly where you are.

Answer the ones that speak to you.
Let yourself free-write, doodle, or simply reflect.

There's no rush.
There's no wrong way.
Just your truth, unfolding on the page.

✎ Pause & Ponder
Return to Center

— *What is one small shift I'm ready to make today—with grace, not pressure?*
— *Where am I being invited to release... and where am I ready to receive?*
— *What has my gut, heart, or head been whispering that I'm ready to hear?*

You've done more than tidy a drawer or mute a distraction.
You've reclaimed your role as the curator of your own life.

You've remembered that your energy is sacred.
That your peace is worth protecting.
That your attention is a powerful form of devotion.

Every choice—what you keep, what you consume, what you invite in—shapes the soil of your becoming.

So let this be your quiet revolution.
Choose what nourishes.
Choose what lights you up.
Choose what brings you home to yourself.

And know this...
You don't have to say yes to everything to live a beautiful life.
You just need to say yes to what matters.

NINE

Let Your Wisdom Guide You

Listening to Your Body, Heart, and Soul

"Sometimes signs are just a tiny whisper in our hearts."
— Laura Lynne Jackson

There comes a moment when the life you've carefully built, through effort, devotion, and years of showing up, starts to feel... off.

Not wrong.
Not broken.
Just no longer quite true.

Maybe it arrives as a quiet discontent or restlessness.
Maybe a question that won't go away.
Maybe as a sense that something deeper is calling, but you're not sure what or why now.

You've done what was asked.
You've held the pieces.
You've made it work.

But now there's a whisper rising:
What do I actually want?
What if this version of my life no longer fits?
What else is possible?

These questions don't come with instructions.
They don't follow timelines.
They don't always make sense, at least not right away.

Because this next chapter?
It won't be found in bullet points or pro/con lists.
It lives in subtler places.
It lives in the *breath* you didn't know you were holding.
In the *tension* that gathers in your shoulders every time you say *yes* when you mean *no*.
In the tears that come when something finally feels aligned.

This is the wisdom of your body.
Of your breath.
Of the part of you that has always known.

Your mind will want to map it.
But your body? She's been holding the coordinates all along.

This chapter isn't here to hand you answers.
It's here to help you return to your truth, to your timing, to your inner knowing.

Because when the noise quiets...
When you pause the performance...
When you soften into presence...

That's when she speaks.

Not the voice of fear or doubt or expectation.
But the voice of you,
the one who trusts, the one who listens, the one who leads.

Let this be your invitation back to her.

Your Body Is the First to Know

If wisdom lives in layers, the body is the first door.
It opens before your mind can catch up, subtle, sacred, sure.

Before your mind can make sense of it,
before the plan is made or the outcome is explained,
your body already knows.

It knows through a flutter in your chest.
A lump in your throat.
A sudden clench in your jaw.
The way you hold your breath in a conversation or exhale fully when you finally feel safe.

These aren't random sensations.
They're signals.
Invitations to pay attention.

But in a world that rewards pushing through, many of us have learned to ignore them.
To override what we feel in the name of what we "should" do.
To stay in rooms our bodies are begging us to leave.
To keep quiet when our chest tightens and our spirit says no.

That disconnection doesn't mean you're broken.
It means you've been conditioned.
And you're not alone.

The good news?
This kind of knowing can be reawakened, gently, intentionally,
one moment at a time.

Your Heart Is Your Guide

If your body is where truth begins,
your heart is where meaning lives.

It doesn't speak in logic.
It speaks in longings.
In ache and yearning.
In resonance and release.

Your heart is where your soul whispers:
This matters. This is love. This is home.

But somewhere along the way,
many of us learned to guard that soft, sacred place.
We built walls.
We played roles.
We got so good at caretaking, performing, and pretending that we forgot how to feel.

We became fluent in *"I'm fine."*
But fine isn't the goal.
Fine isn't joy.
Fine isn't presence.
Fine isn't *fully alive.*

Your heart wasn't made to settle.
It was made to beat wildly for what moves you.
To soften when something real arrives.
To break open and then stretch wider with compassion.

This chapter is a gentle homecoming.

A return to what makes your heart feel full.
A moment to notice what stirs emotion in you, not to fix it, but to honor it.

Maybe it's the swell in your chest when you hear your child's laughter.
The lump in your throat when a friend holds space for your grief.
The warm ache of longing when you remember a version of yourself you've left behind.

These are not distractions.
They're directions.

Your heart is a compass.
It points toward what matters.

So the question becomes:
Are you making space to feel it?
Or are you busy managing everything else?

Feeling deeply isn't a weakness.
It's strength wrapped in softness.
It's wisdom in motion.

Let yourself cry.
Let yourself care.
Let yourself get goosebumps from a song, chills from a poem, or a heart swell beneath a glorious blue sky.

These are not random.
They're *reminders*.
That you are still here.
Still open.
Still capable of love, of wonder, of deep knowing.

Let this be a season of tending.
Of turning inward.
Of listening to the rhythms of your own heart.

Because when you honor what moves you,
you remember who you really are.

And when you begin to follow it, even hesitantly,
it often leads you somewhere deeper, truer, more aligned with your soul.

And in that remembering, wisdom returns.
Not in noise, but in symbols.
Not in facts, but in stories.

Let me share one of mine.

The Wisdom Within

Long ago, the elders gathered with a sacred question:
Where should we hide the truth of life?
The sacred wisdom. The deep knowing.
The guidance that would lead future generations home.

One elder said:
"Let's place it in the belly of a great whale, deep in the ocean. Let them dive into the depths of their intuition to find it."

Another said:
"No, let's tuck it into the heart of an elephant, steady, strong, and full of memory. Let them return to love to remember who they are."

A third offered:
"Better still, let's hide it in the mind of an eagle, far above the clouds. Let them rise, and rise again, to see clearly."

But the eldest among them paused, then smiled and said:
*"No. Let's place it in the one place they'll forget to look...
Within.*

For only when they trust their gut, soften into their heart, and quiet their mind will they remember they've had it all along."

I wrote that story in a moment of sacred stillness.
No overthinking. No striving. Just presence.

And then, something extraordinary happened.

I walked out to my backyard, letting the words settle into my soul.

And suddenly, soaring above me, a bald eagle appeared.
It circled my property once.
Then again.
Then a third time.

And with a final screech—raw, wild, undeniable—it flew off.

I stood there, barefoot in the grass...
stunned, undone, and overflowing with quiet wonder.

Grateful. Speechless. Deeply aware of just how sacred life can be.
The parable wasn't just a story.
It was a message.
A moment of absolute alignment.
A gentle, divine nudge that I was on the right path.

A whisper from the universe saying:
Keep going. This matters.

It feels vulnerable to share something so personal.
And I offer it not to impress, or to prove,
only to remind *you* of what becomes possible
when we open our hearts to something greater than ourselves.

There's wisdom that lives within each of us.
It's always been there, quiet, steady, waiting.
And the more we listen, the more clearly it speaks.

Listen Beyond Logic

Some truths don't come from thinking.
They come from noticing.

From the chills that rise before your brain understands why.
From the nudge that tells you to turn left instead of right.
From the flicker of recognition when something just feels aligned.

In a world that prizes logic, intuition often gets dismissed.
But intuition isn't fluff. It's not indulgent. It's not a luxury.
It's ancient. Sacred. Essential.

It's the soft inner voice that remembers what your soul came here to do.
You might call it instinct. Spirit. Higher Self.

You might experience it through dreams, synchronicities, or stillness.
It doesn't need a label, it only asks that you listen.

I call them **Divine Nudges**—those gentle whispers, well-timed signs, or subtle
winks that remind us we're not alone.
That something wiser is walking with us.
That the path is unfolding, even when we can't yet see around the bend.

Maybe it's a song that plays at just the right moment.
A memory that returns when you need it most.
A shiver or goosebumps that rise without warning.
A dragonfly or a ladybug that appears just when you ask for a sign.
A number that keeps repeating, softly, consistently,
until you finally pause to notice.

They're easy to miss in a world that moves fast,
expects you to push,
and rarely teaches you to listen.

But when you slow down,
when you soften, breathe, and begin to pay attention,
you'll start to notice.

And that noticing?
That's the beginning of remembering.

You get to name this knowing in whatever way feels true to you.
For some, it's Spirit. Or God. Or intuition.
For others, it's nature, rhythm, or the voice within.
You don't need to define it.
You just need to listen for it.

They're not random.
They're invitations. Confirmations.
Quiet echoes of something greater saying, *"This matters. Keep going."*

Want to deepen your awareness?
Try this simple practice.

Pause and close your eyes.
Place one hand on your heart, one on your belly.
Take three slow breaths.

Ask:
Is there something I'm being shown right now?
Something I've been too busy to notice?

Then... wait.
Learn to be with silence a little longer.
Don't force it. Just *feel*.
Whatever comes—an image, a word, a tear, a memory—is enough.

You don't need to chase clarity.
You just need to create space for it to arrive.

Soften the grip on certainty.
Quiet the noise.
Notice the gentle ways your life is already speaking to you.

Because the truth is:
You are deeply guided.
You are lovingly held.
And the wisdom you seek?
It's already within you, whispering back:
Yes, love... this way.

You've opened. You've listened.
You've remembered what it feels like to be guided from within.

Now, let your body rest. Let it integrate.

The following practices are here to help you soften, reconnect, and gently return to your center, no pressure, no performance, just presence.

Pick one. Or slowly try them all over time.
Let these be sacred pauses in your day, or soft landings in your week.

Because sometimes, *rest is the most powerful choice.*

☀︎᷈ Inspired Practice
5-4-3-2-1 Grounding

Sometimes the simplest way to reconnect with your body is to return to your senses, literally.

This practice helps you settle into the present by guiding you from what's most external (sight) to what's most internal (taste). Think of it as a gentle descent—from the world around you, into the world within you.

When things feel loud, fast, or overwhelming, try this:

5 things you can see
Look around. Notice five things you can see.
The shape of your hands. A window. A candle. The texture of the wall.
The color of your socks.

4 things you can touch
Now notice four things you can touch.
The fabric of your clothes. The chair beneath you. Your palms resting in your lap.
Your feet on the floor.

3 things you can hear
Listen for three distinct sounds.
The hum of a heater. A bird outside. Your breath moving in and out. Silence, even.

2 things you can smell
Bring your attention closer in.
Maybe your shampoo or the faint scent of the room you're in.
And if you can't smell anything right now, that's okay, just notice that too.

1 thing you can taste
Notice what lingers.
A sip of water. Coffee. Toothpaste. Your own saliva. Nothing at all.
Simply observe without judgment.

Every single time I do this practice, something in me settles.
My breath deepens. My body softens. My nervous system unclenches.

I feel more present.
More aligned.
More... here.

This practice won't solve everything.
However, it brings you back to now.
And sometimes, now is exactly where the healing begins.

☀︎〜 Inspired Practice
Tense and Relax

We don't always realize how much tension we're holding until we're invited to let it go.

This gentle, grounding practice guides you through a full-body scan, tensing and releasing one muscle group at a time. It's especially helpful when your nervous system feels tight—after a long day, before bed, or in that moment you realize your shoulders are close to your ears.

It's not about *forcing* relaxation; it's about *inviting* it, one breath at a time.

Starting from your feet and moving up helps root your awareness in the present moment, where your breath and truth reside.

Choose a position—lying down or seated—that feels supportive.

For each area of your body, you'll gently tense the muscles for about 5–10 seconds, then release. Let the release be complete. Don't ease out slowly. Let it drop. Let it go.

Begin with a few deep breaths. Then, slowly and intentionally:

Feet
Curl your toes as if gripping a flip-flop.
Then release—let them flop.

Legs
Squeeze your calves and thighs like you're bracing for cold water.
Then let go—allow gravity to soften your legs.

Hips and Booty
Squeeze your hips and booty. Brace as if bouncing on a trampoline.
Then release—let go completely. Allow yourself to be held.

Stomach and Back
Gently draw your belly inward. Pause.
Then let it go—feel your low back soften and melt into the earth.

Hands and Arms

Clench your fists and draw your arms close. Hold that quiet embrace.
Stretch your fingers wide, widening the space.
Then soften—release into ease, invite peace in.

Shoulders

Draw your shoulders up toward your ears—just a little closer to your ears.
Then let them fall. The weight of the world was never yours to carry.

Face, Jaw, Neck, and Tongue

Scrunch your face—tighten your jaw, open your eyes and mouth wide, stick
out your tongue as if touching your chin. Hold.
Now fully release: let your face go slack, tongue drop, and neck soften
completely.

Pause and linger here a little longer.
Notice the difference.

Maybe it's the weight of your limbs.
Maybe it's the quiet in your chest.
Maybe it's just a little more space inside your breath.

Let that be enough.

You don't have to rush back.
You don't have to do anything next.
You've already done something powerful.
You came home to your body.

When you're ready... come back slowly.

And know you can return to this practice anytime you need a reset—
before bed,
after a long day,
or whenever your shoulders are creeping back toward your ears.

☀︎∿ Inspired Practice
Body Scan

There's a quiet kind of knowing that lives in your body.
Not loud. Not pushy. Just... waiting. Patiently.

This practice invites you into gentle awareness, slow, soul-soothing, and without agenda.
It's not about fixing or changing anything.
It's about witnessing.
Being with what is.

Perfect for moments when you feel disconnected or distant from yourself, this simple scan helps you return to your body with tenderness and care.
A soft landing.
A sacred pause.

Let yourself be here. Without pressure. Without performance. Just presence.

Lie down if that feels good.
Or sit somewhere soft.
Let your spine lengthen, but not in a way that performs.
In a way *that remembers.*

Close your eyes, if you'd like.
Take a deep breath in.
And as you exhale, let your awareness drop,
down from the swirl of the day,
down into the quiet hum of your body.

Begin at your **feet**.
You don't have to name what you feel.
Just notice.
The weight. The warmth. The stillness. The something.

Move slowly into your **legs**.
Let your attention drape across your calves, your knees, your thighs.

What's here?
Can you meet it without needing to label it?

Bring awareness to your **hips and seat**.
The place that holds you. Anchors you.
Let it feel held.

Now your **belly and lower back**.
Maybe there's movement. Maybe not.
Let it be. Let it soften.

Feel into your **chest and upper back**.
The rhythm of breath. The rise and fall.
The beating of a heart that's carried so much.

Let your attention flow into your **arms and hands**.
From your shoulders to your elbows to your fingertips.
Can you feel your edges soften?

Now your **neck,** your **jaw,** your **face**.
Release your tongue from the roof of your mouth.
Let your brow smooth.
Let your expression fall away.

And just rest here.
In this quiet body.
In this quiet now.

Nothing to do.
Nothing to earn.
Just a moment to be fully in yourself.

☀∿ Inspired Practice
Somatic Compass

Your body often knows the answer before your mind can explain it.
Before logic kicks in.
Before words arrive.
Your body whispers.

It speaks in sensations:
A racing heart.
Tight shoulders.
A lump in your throat.
A flutter in your belly.
Goosebumps rising out of nowhere.
A truth that hits the air differently the moment you say it aloud.
A full-bodied exhale that seems to rise from your bones.

These aren't just symptoms.
They're signals.
Truth markers.
Inner wisdom rising.

But in a world that rewards pushing through, we've been taught to override those signals.
We dismiss the ache in our chest when we're with the wrong people.
We ignore the ease in our breath when something is right.
But these aren't just passing feelings—they're communicating truth.
Inviting us to notice and know.

Your body remembers.

It remembers who you are.
It remembers what's true.
It remembers what it feels like to move through the world in alignment.

Whether you're barefoot on the earth,
dancing wildly in your living room,

or weeping in child's pose,
your body leads the way.
Not with words, but with wisdom.

This is where movement becomes more than physical.
It becomes *medicine, memory, a map.*
A sacred way home to yourself.

It might look like:

- Shaking out stress when words fall short.
- Stretching until tears surface and your breath softens.
- Walking without a destination, letting your steps untangle your thoughts.
- Sitting in stillness and realizing you've finally exhaled.

There's no one right way to move with intention, only *your* way.
And it begins not by asking, *"What should I do?"*
but by listening to, *"What is my body asking for?"*

There's no universal code, only *your* code.
And the more you listen, the louder your truth becomes.

For some, a "yes" feels like warmth.
Or lightness.
Or grounded peace.
It might show up as a spontaneous smile,
a sense of ease in your breath,
or a quiet rising in your chest,
like your body is leaning in before your mind can explain why.

A "no" might feel like tightness.
A pit in your stomach.
A shallow breath.
Tension in your shoulders,
A quiet urge to step back,
shake your head,
or slowly retreat without knowing why.

We call this your **Somatic Compass**, the inner language of your body that guides you toward alignment.

These patterns aren't just intuitive; they're also supported by science.
People often look **up** when accessing logic or visuals.
We look **down** when connecting to emotion.
To the **left** to recall memories.
To the **right** to imagine or create.
These patterns are more than habits. They're echoes of your deepest wisdom—
what science now supports and what your body has always whispered:
You hold the answers within.

Want to practice tuning in? Start here.
Find a quiet space.
Sit comfortably.
Place your feet on the ground.
Close your eyes, if that feels safe.
Take a few slow, steady breaths.

Begin with something true.
Say out loud: *"My name is [your name]."*
Notice your body's response.

Now speak something untrue.
Say: *"My name is [a different name]."*
Again, observe what shifts.

Maybe your breath caught.
Maybe your posture changed.
Maybe you simply felt the difference.

Now try it with a question your heart has been holding:
"This job is right for me."
"I want to move to that city."
"I'm ready for this relationship."
"I am meant to live in peace."

Say each one slowly.
Let the words land.
And let your body speak before your brain rushes in.

This is how we begin to remember our inner language.
Not by fixing or forcing.
But by feeling.
By listening.
By trusting the wisdom that lives beneath the noise.

You don't always need a spreadsheet to make your next decision.
You need a moment of stillness.
A breath.
And a willingness to listen.

Let this be your practice, not to control your body,
but to trust it.
Not to push it harder,
but to partner with it.
Not to fix it,
but to come home to it.

☀〰 Inspired Practice
Draw Yourself

Take 10–15 minutes to draw yourself on the next page. That's it. No rules. No explanations. Just you, as you are, however that looks today. Use whatever tools you have nearby (pen, pencil, marker, crayon). Don't overthink it.

This isn't about accuracy. It isn't about beauty. It isn't about artistic ability. It's simply a way to notice what comes through when you put pen to paper.

If you're curious about what your drawing might reveal, scan the QR code below or visit drdeonne.com/draw

There, you'll find a gentle invitation to explore what your drawing may be trying to tell you, from proportions to presence, from posture to what's quietly asking to be seen.

And remember: *sometimes, the soul speaks in symbols before it ever finds words.*

Scan the QR code to access
Beyond the Drawing
or visit drdeonne.com/draw

✎ Pause & Ponder
Listen to Your Body's Wisdom

Your body has always been whispering.
Now is your chance to listen.

Let this be less about answers and more about honesty.
Let your pen move. Let your truth rise.

— *What does a full-bodied "yes" feel like for you? And how does your body say "no?"*
— *When has your body known the truth before your mind could catch up?*
— *Where are you being asked to trust your own wisdom more deeply, more boldly?*

✎ Pause & Ponder
Trust the Winks and Whispers

The world is speaking to you.
Through signs. Symbols. Synchronicities.

Not everything has to make sense right away.
Let this be a space to notice what's been quietly guiding you all along.

— *What signs or "coincidences" have shown up in your life lately?*
— *If you were to choose a personal symbol of love, presence, or divine reassurance, what would it be?*
— *What helps you slow down enough to notice the magic all around you?*

☀︎⌁ Inspired Practice
Yoga Nidra

There is a kind of rest your body rarely receives.
A rest so deep, it asks nothing of you, not even sleep.

Yoga Nidra means "yogic sleep," but this isn't about drifting off.
It's about surrender. Integration. A dreamy, feminine stillness that restores you from the inside out.

This practice invites you into sacred rest, the kind that supports your nervous system, softens your edges, and helps your body heal without effort. You'll be guided into that in-between space, where your breath moves on its own, your body releases what it's been holding, and your mind finally lets go.

You don't need to do anything.
You don't even need to stay alert.
Just lie down. Listen. Receive.

There's no pose. No stretching. No performance.
Just stillness. Just presence. Just the sound of a voice walking you gently back to yourself.

This is a practice of receiving.
Of allowing healing to happen without your control.
Of remembering what it feels like to be safe... to be still... to be whole.

Let this be your sacred rest.
Not earned. Not delayed.
But offered. Now.

You've just remembered how to listen to your body,
not as something to fix or control,
but as a sacred source of truth.

You've softened into your heart,
the quiet space where compassion lives,
where intuition roots itself in love.

You've begun to notice the divine nudges,
the whispers, the winks,
the gentle reminders that you're never alone.

These aren't separate voices.
They're one voice—**yours**.
Different expressions of the same deep knowing.

Your body.
Your heart.
Your spirit.

All speaking in their own language,
All guiding you back home to yourself.

And now that you've reconnected with that wisdom,
the truth beneath the noise,
you're ready for what's next.

Because the path forward isn't paved with pressure.
It's shaped by small, sacred steps rooted in alignment.

Let's explore what it means to move from knowing... to doing.

One breath.
One choice.
One brave, beautiful step at a time.

Bring these practices off the page and into your daily rhythm. Access guided meditations for this chapter by scanning the QR code below.

Scan the QR code to listen to
Guided Meditations
or visit drdeonne.com/meditations

TEN

Aligned Action

Gentle Rhythms Toward Who You're Becoming

"Don't ask what the world needs. Ask what makes you come alive and go do it."
— Howard Thurman

You don't need another to-do list.
You need a way to become the woman you're already envisioning.

This chapter is about action,
but not the kind that burns you out or pulls you away from yourself.
It's about aligned action: small, soul-matching steps that move you forward
without losing your center.

Action is the bridge from intention to transformation.

Not hustle.
Not perfection.
But courageous, consistent choices that reflect your inner clarity.

You're invited to explore three soul-centered questions:
What's ready to begin?
What's ready to be released?
And what deserves to keep growing?

Then, we'll map out daily anchors:
not rigid routines, but sacred rhythms that honor your energy and intention.
Morning practices that help you begin with clarity.
Evening rituals that return you to calm.

This is where you stop performing and start practicing.
Where you stop proving and start embodying.

Start. Stop. Continue.

Some of the most powerful shifts begin with just three simple words:
Start. Stop. Continue.

This framework has been a longtime favorite of mine, something I used while managing a large team, and now in my personal life and coaching practice.

It's a tool rooted in clarity. *Not perfection.*
It invites you to get honest, *without shame,* about what's working, what's not, and what's quietly asking to emerge.

When I used this framework with my team, I handed out small slips of paper and asked everyone to write down what we should start doing, stop doing, and continue doing. No names. No explanations. Just radical honesty. We grouped the responses by theme and talked openly about what was aligned—and what wasn't.

Now, I've adapted it for my own life.
Here's how it looks:

Start
I want to start strengthening my morning practice.
Not to hustle harder, but to root deeper.

Gentle movement.
A cup of tea.
A consistent journaling practice with the prompt:
"Dear One, what would you have me know today?"

Simple rhythms that ground me in who I am and who I'm becoming.

Stop
This one takes courage. But I'm willing to go there.

For me, one practice I'm ready to stop is *overconsuming social media*.
Not because it's inherently bad, but because sometimes I use it to numb.

And maybe you're numb too.

Whether it's food, alcohol, scrolling, overworking, or perfectionism,
so many of us use something to disconnect from ourselves.

This isn't about shame.
It's about awareness.

Ask yourself:
Is this behavior creating the life I want?
Does it align with my Dream Life Grid?
My Vision Board?
My Dream Life Audio?

Continue
Here's the beautiful part: some things are already working.
You don't need to change everything.

For me, I want to continue nurturing my core values.
Especially *adventure*—big and small.
That might mean a plane ticket to somewhere new
or just taking a different path on my morning walk.

I want to continue feeding what lights me up.
Because *joy is fuel*.
And the life I'm creating runs on joy.

☀︎〰 𝗜𝗻𝘀𝗽𝗶𝗿𝗲𝗱 𝗣𝗿𝗮𝗰𝘁𝗶𝗰𝗲
𝗦𝘁𝗮𝗿𝘁. 𝗦𝘁𝗼𝗽. 𝗖𝗼𝗻𝘁𝗶𝗻𝘂𝗲.

Take a deep breath.
Place a hand on your heart, or your belly, or both.
Close your eyes for a moment. Tune in.

Ask yourself gently:
— *What's asking to begin?*
— *What's ready to be released?*
— *What wants to be honored and carried forward?*

Then write freely.
Let it flow. Let it be real. Let it be yours.

Start: What do you want to invite in?
Stop: What's no longer aligned with your becoming?
Continue: What's already working that you want to nourish and protect?

You don't need a five-year plan.
You just need presence and one step.

Come back to this practice anytime you feel stuck, scattered, or uncertain.
It's not about doing more.
It's about doing what matters.

☀︎〰 Inspired Practice
Start

— *What is quietly calling to be added to your life?*
— *A new habit, a slight shift, a dream long tucked away?*
— *What do I want to start doing to supports the life I'm creating?*

☀︎〰 Inspired Practice
Stop

— *What is no longer aligned?*
— *What patterns, distractions, or behaviors are ready to be released with grace?*
— *What have I been holding onto that's quietly holding me back?*

☀︎〰 Inspired Practice
Continue

— *What is working beautifully in your life right now?*
— *What lights you up? Grounds you? Keeps you rooted in who you are becoming?*
— *What do I want to continue because it aligns with my values, joy, and vision?*
— *What would my future self thank me for continuing today?*
— *What small action today supports the life you're dreaming into being?*

Daily Anchors

Your day begins before you get out of bed.
It starts with how you greet yourself in the quiet.
With how you open, not just your eyes, but your heart.

I've come to think of mornings as a sacred doorway,
a gentle place to remember who I am before the world rushes in.

Some days, my practice is simple:
A hand on my heart, another on my belly. A breath. A whispered thank you for
what lies ahead.
That's enough. That's gentle.

Other days, I lean into more:
A slow yoga flow or a barefoot walk outside, letting the sunlight touch my skin
and anchor my nervous system.
Reading something that nourishes my soul.
Journaling with my favorite question, *"Dear One, what would you have me know
today?"* (Yes, you've seen this prompt before. Yes, it's worth repeating.)

Some mornings it's five quiet minutes.
On other days, it stretches to two hours.
There's no perfect formula.
No gold star for doing it all.

When I'm fully aligned, stretched into the highest version of myself,
I'm doing all the things:
Movement.
Meditation.
Reading.
Writing.
And gratitude—always, gratitude.

Not because I have to,
but because I *want* to.
Because I know how good it feels
to live from that place of clarity and peace.

This isn't about achieving the *perfect* morning.
It's about honoring your rhythm.
Aligning with your energy.
And beginning your day rooted in truth.

And just as morning sets the tone, your evening can be a soft return.

My own evening ritual is simple, but powerful:
I pick up a small amethyst stone from my nightstand and place it on my heart.
Then I ask myself one question:
"What was the very best thing that happened today?"

And I reflect with intentionality and playfulness.
I mentally replay the day and weigh the beauty of each moment.
Was it the conversation with a friend?
The laughter in the kitchen?
The peaceful walk at sunset?
Which one was the very best?

I call it the **Gratitude Game.**
A celebration of presence.
A nightly practice of remembering the good.

But you don't need to copy mine.
You get to create your own.
Your rhythm. Your practice.
Your sacred anchors.

☀︎〜 Inspired Practice
Daily Anchors

Design a rhythm that supports your becoming.
On the following two pages, sketch out your morning and evening anchors.
Not productivity for productivity's sake, but sacred bookends to hold your day
with intention.

Use the **Gentle—Ideal—Stretch** framework to support your thinking:

Morning Practice:
How do you want to feel when you start your day? Then connect with the
feeling as if it were already here.
For example, do you want to start your day with presence and clarity? What
would support that start?

Evening Ritual:
How do you want to feel when you end your day? Then connect with the
feeling as if it were already here.
For example, do you want to end with peace and gratitude? What would help
you return to this feeling?

Gentle: The smallest, kindest step you could take
Ideal: A rhythm that feels like you
Stretch: The full embodiment of your dream life

No pressure. No perfect routine.
Just honest and flexible support for the life you're ready to live.

Let this be your invitation to bookend your days
with practices that support your *body, your mind, and your soul.*

 **Inspired Practice**
Morning Practice

 Inspired Practice
Evening Ritual

You've just made space for honest reflection.
You named what's working.
You released what's no longer aligned.
And you gave voice to what's ready to emerge.

These aren't routines to perfect.
They're practices of devotion.

Keep honoring the small steps.
The morning breath.
The evening exhale.
The moment you choose alignment over autopilot.

You've done the work.
You've reflected, realigned, and rooted into what matters.
Let that be enough.
Let that be beautiful.
Let that be your next step.

ELEVEN

Eyes on the Good

Gratitude as a Practice of Perspective, Power, and Presence

*"Acknowledging the good that you already have in your life
is the foundation for all abundance."*

— Eckhart Tolle

Gratitude is the sacred thread that stitches the soul to the present moment.
It brings us home to what is.
To what's already enough.
To what's quietly waiting to be seen.

Gratitude isn't about bypassing pain or pretending things are perfect.
It's about intentionally choosing to see through a different lens:
one that reveals *peace, presence, and possibility,*
beyond our hard-wired negativity bias.

When you practice gratitude, you soften your edges.
You open your heart.
You gently shift your perspective from *lack to love.*

And sometimes, the most profound way to move forward...
is a simple act of kindness.

Random Acts of Kindness

There's research that confirms what we already know within:
when a **random act of kindness** is given, the giver feels good,
the receiver feels good—and here's the beautiful part—so does the observer.

Just witnessing kindness has its own quiet power. It lifts the room, softens the
walls that are up, and brings *humanity back into the moment.*

A few years ago, after reading that study, I found myself standing in line at a
Starbucks in the airport. Behind me, a woman was juggling a baby, a stroller,
and a toddler trying to eat oatmeal. The barista had forgotten his spoon, and
the mother looked... done. We've all been there.

So I asked for a spoon and handed it to the little one.
That's it.
That's the whole story.

But something shifted. The air softened. People smiled. Tension melted.
All because of one tiny act.

You never know who's watching. You never know how far your ripple will go.

☀·⌇ Inspired Practice
Random Acts of Kindness

Kindness is magic—and it multiplies.

Start your own list of Random Acts of Kindness.
Not to earn a gold star, but to sprinkle light wherever you go.

Need a few ideas?

- Pay for the person behind you in line
- Compliment someone in the grocery store
- Leave quarters at the laundromat
- Tip big, just because
- Send a book to someone who needs it
- Tuck handwritten notes into library books or backpacks
- Babysit for a tired parent
- Mail a thank-you card to someone who's shaped your life

Add your own.

Make it playful. Make it soulful.

More acts, more magic—what kindness is still waiting to be shared?

Gratitude for Others

This is often the easiest doorway in,
the most accessible and the most immediate.

Think of someone who made your life a little brighter.
A teacher who saw you.
A friend who showed up.
A stranger who made you feel less alone in a hard moment.
Someone who didn't need to—but did anyway.

Let yourself remember them.
Not just the moment, but how it made you feel.
The warmth. The safety. The sense of being seen.

Maybe it was recent.
Maybe it was decades ago.
Either way, that imprint lives in you.

Write a few names.
A few memories.
A few thank yous.

Let this be a pause of acknowledgment—for those who stood beside you in quiet, meaningful ways.

And if your heart nudges you to reach out, to tell them what they meant, follow that nudge.

Because gratitude doesn't just warm the giver and the receiver.
It reminds us that we were never walking alone.

Let this be your whisper of thanks:
I remember.
I receive.
I'm grateful.

Gratitude for Self

Now let's turn inward.

This part might feel unfamiliar.
Even uncomfortable.
Because gratitude for self is often the *last* place we look.

You've spent years showing up for others.
Tending. Soothing. Fixing.
You've celebrated their wins. Softened their falls. Held space for their becoming.

But what about you?

What about the woman who keeps going, even when no one sees the cost?
What about the one who doubts, but rises anyway?
The one who holds grace and grief in the same breath?

You deserve your own thank you.

Not because you've been perfect.
But because you've been *true*.
Because you are still here—becoming, unbecoming, becoming again.

Think of a quality you admire in others.
Compassion. Grit. Humor. Wisdom.

You notice it for a reason, because it already lives in you.
As they say, "*If you spot it, you got it.*"

Pause.
Can you let that truth in? Just a little?

You are not too much.
You are not behind.
You are not broken.

You are becoming.
And that deserves reverence.

So tonight, or sometime soon, let your heart speak:
Thank you for carrying me through.
I'm proud of who you are and who you're becoming.
I'm still learning to love you, and I won't stop trying.

This isn't self-indulgence.
This is self-honoring.
And it's how we begin to build a life rooted in truth.

Because here's the secret:
When you can see the good in *yourself*—not just in others—everything starts
to shift.

The way you speak.
The choices you make.
The love you allow.
The dreams you dare to hold.

This is where transformation takes root.
Not in trying harder.
But in softening toward yourself.

Let that be your medicine tonight.

Gratitude for Life

This is where things may get more challenging and deeper.
Because it's one thing to be grateful for what's good.
It's another to find gratitude in the *hard stuff.*

But here's the quiet truth:
Some of the most meaningful transformations in our lives are born from
moments we never would have chosen.

Loss.
Failure.
Transition.

Loneliness.
The gut-wrenching seasons when the map disappears and we're left holding only questions.

It's okay if you're not grateful for those things.
But can you soften toward what they made possible?

Maybe they cracked you open.
Maybe they stripped away what was never truly yours.
Maybe they showed you who you are when everything else fell away.

That's sacred. That's growth.
And honoring that doesn't mean bypassing the pain,
it means blessing what it built.

A few years ago, I had a difficult Thanksgiving.
I felt the weight of disconnection, grief, and change heavy in my chest.
And I knew I had a choice: spiral into sadness... or do something different.

So I made a list of 100 people who had impacted my life.
Friends. Family. Former students. Colleagues. Mentors.

Each message was unique. Personal. From the heart.
And something wild happened.

My heart filled.
The loneliness softened.
Gratitude alchemized it all.

Because sometimes, the fastest way to feel love... is to give it.

Gratitude opened the door—from isolation to connection, from sadness to meaning.

I gave love away that day. And in doing so, I found myself again.

✎ Pause & Ponder
Catching Beauty in the Everyday

Take a moment to slow down and reflect.
Not because you have to,
but because your heart deserves it.

There are no rules here. Just write what rises.

You might begin with:
— *What am I grateful for in others, and how have they shaped me?*
— *What part of myself deserves more appreciation, more softness?*
— *Where in my story can I find gratitude for the journey of becoming?*

And if you feel called:
Write a letter. Send a text. Record an audio message.
To someone who changed your life.
To yourself.
To life itself.

Let it be whatever form feels most true.
Whatever way your heart wants to speak.

Send it... or don't.
Sometimes the writing *is* the ritual.

You've practiced noticing what's good.
You've remembered that you're part of something bigger.
You've even dared to give thanks for the hard things—the ones that shaped you, stretched you, and brought you here.

Gratitude is more than a moment.
It's a way of seeing.
A way of softening.
A way of living.

This isn't the end of your gratitude practice.
It's the beginning of a new lens.
A new rhythm.
A new relationship with joy.

And as we step into our final chapter of this journey together, let this be your foundation:

You don't have to become someone else to live a beautiful life.
You only have to come home to the one who's been here all along.

TWELVE

You're Not Behind, You're Becoming

Honoring the Sacred Pace of Who You're Becoming

"You're playing small does not serve the world. There is nothing enlightened about shrinking so that other people won't feel insecure."

— Marianne Williamson

You've shifted.
You've softened.
You've strengthened.

This is a sacred moment...
to reflect, to anchor, to name the woman you're becoming.

Not because the journey is over,
but because you've come far enough to see how far you've come.

There's something I want to share with you.
A quiet metaphor for transformation that lives in nature.

The Bamboo Way

When bamboo is planted, nothing seems to happen for years.
You water it. Nurture it. Show up for it.
And still, nothing breaks the surface.

To most eyes, it looks like failure.
Like stillness.
Like waiting.

But underground, the roots are growing.
Expanding. Strengthening.
Quietly building the foundation needed to support what's coming.

And then—when the time is right—it rises.

Fast. Strong. Unapologetically tall.

Some species of bamboo can grow more than **three feet in a single day.**
That's not a typo.
It's one of the fastest-growing plants on Earth.

But it only grows that quickly *after* years of unseen preparation.
That's the part most people miss.

Maybe that's you.

Maybe that's what *all of this* has been.
The inner work.
The invisible shifts.
The quiet choices no one else saw.

Maybe you weren't stuck...
Maybe you were becoming.

You've met yourself with compassion, courage, and clarity.
You've listened more deeply. Moved more intentionally.
You've remembered your truth.

And now, it's time.

Throughout these pages, you've been remembering her—the wise, grounded, joyful you who has always been walking beside you.

And now... you get to meet her.

Some call her their Higher Self.
Others call her Future Me.
You might call her your Wise Woman, your Inner Guide.

Or maybe, for the first time,
you'll call her by your own name... and mean it differently.

The "future" version of you.
She's wise. Grounded. Free. Joyful. Radiant.

She is not waiting—she is walking beside you.
She always has been.

This chapter is your invitation to connect with her.
To let her speak.
To let her guide.
To feel her presence as your quiet knowing,
your steady courage,
your unapologetic joy.

You don't have to strive to become her.
You simply get to remember,
you already are.

And now, with deeper roots and clearer eyes,
you return to where you began,
not to measure progress,
but to witness your becoming.

This isn't just another exercise.
This is a moment of truth.

☀︎〜 Inspired Practice
Your Bloomprint Revisited

At the beginning of this journey, you completed your first Bloomprint.
You looked at where your energy was going, where it was missing,
and what was quietly asking to be seen.

That first reflection didn't define you.
It simply offered you a snapshot, a starting point.

Since then, you've done the work.
You've paused long enough to listen inward.
You've created space. You've cleared the clutter.
You've uncovered your values and explored what truly matters.

You've softened the voice of your inner critic.
You've extended compassion to yourself and others.
You've rewritten outdated stories.

You've honored your intuition, tended your body,
and made room for joy, stillness, and divine nudges.
You've clarified your vision, spoken your dreams aloud,
and taken gentle, powerful steps toward becoming.

This hasn't been a surface-level change.
This has been courageous, soul-level reclamation.

You've chosen to look within,
not for what's broken,
but for what's always been whole.

That deserves to be seen.
That deserves to be celebrated.

This is your moment to pause and reflect.
To measure growth by awareness, not symmetry,
To celebrate how it feels to live inside your life.

Take a look at your original Bloomprint.
What's shifted? What feels lighter, fuller, more grounded?

There's no pass or fail here—only reflection, only truth.

Below you'll find a blank Bloomprint. Take your time.
Fill it in honestly, intuitively. Notice what feels different from when you began.

Then pause. Celebrate what's grown.

Because you didn't just complete a book.
You chose yourself—again and again.

And that changes everything.

✎ ⌒ Pause & Ponder
An Invitation to Reflect

Now that you've completed your updated Bloomprint, take a breath. This isn't about reaching perfection. It's about honoring your becoming. Let these questions gently guide your reflection:

— *What feels different from the first time you completed this?*
— *Where do you notice the most growth or healing?*
— *What surprised you, in a good way?*
— *What's still calling for your attention, care, or intention?*
— *How does this version of your life feel compared to before?*

You don't need to answer everything right now. This page is simply an invitation to witness your progress. Deeper reflection lives on the next page.

A Letter from Your Future Self

Take a breath.
Deeper than the last.
Let it fill your belly, your chest, your soul.

Now exhale. Slowly.
Softly.
Let go of the noise, the rushing, the to-do list.

This moment isn't about what you should be doing.
It's about who you're becoming.

Close your eyes, if that feels good.
Place one hand on your heart.
And if it helps, the other on your belly.

Feel your body.
Feel the ground beneath you.
Feel the quiet strength that's always lived inside you.

Now imagine her.
The future version of you.

Not a fantasy.
Not a Pinterest-perfect version.
But the one who's healing
The one who trusts herself.
The one who moves through life with clarity and ease.
The one who walks barefoot in her truth and knows she is enough.

See her.
Where is she?
What does her space feel like?
What does she know that you're still learning to believe?

Is she older? Wiser? Playful? Soft? Fierce?
What's she wearing?

What's in her hands?
What knowing lives in her eyes?

Take your time.
There's no rush.

When she's ready, she'll speak.
Maybe it's a whisper.
Maybe it's a flood.
Maybe it's just a few truthful words.

But this... this is sacred space.
This is where remembering happens.

Let her write to you.
Let her remind you of what matters.
Let her celebrate what you've just done,
the courage, the clarity, the pages you've filled.

Let her offer love.
Let her offer grace.
Let her say the words you've been longing to hear.

This is not a performance.
This is not a test.
This is a homecoming.

Let her guide your pen.
Let her tell you who you already are.

✎ Pause & Ponder
A Letter from Your Future Self

Let this be a love note from your higher self,
the you who trusts, who remembers, who knows you're already enough.

Use one of these as your first line:
— *I'm so proud of you for...*
— *You're learning to trust...*
— *I see how far you've come, even when you can't...*

Let her voice come through your pen.
Let it feel like a homecoming.

☀〰 Inspired Practice
Light It. Wear It. Write It.

You've done the inner work.
Now, let your body and space hold that knowing.

Choose one—or all—of the invitations below to mark your becoming:

Light It
Create a quiet moment just for you.
Light a candle. Let the flame reflect the fire within you.
Say aloud,
"I honor who I've been, who I am, and who I'm becoming.
May my light guide others home to themselves."

Wear It
Choose something meaningful to wear—a piece of jewelry, a color, a scarf, a crystal, a scent.
Let it carry the energy of your journey—your strength, your softness, your sacred becoming.
Each time you wear it, let it remind you of who you are... and who you're becoming.

Write It
Craft a vow to yourself. Begin with, *"I vow to..."*
Keep it visible.
In your journal. On your mirror. Tucked into your wallet.
Let it guide you back to what matters.

This is your rite of remembrance.
You're not the same woman who began this book.
And the most beautiful part?
You're still becoming.

You never needed to be fixed.
You just needed to remember.

Remember who you are beneath the exhaustion, the roles, the relentless expectations.
This journey has never been about becoming someone new;
it's always been about coming home to yourself.

Through these pages, you've traced the places your energy was leaking.
You've questioned the stories that no longer serve you.
You've found your way back—gently, honestly, powerfully.

You've rewritten old stories.
You've reflected with honesty and heart.
You've risen—softly, steadily.
You've reclaimed your energy, joy, and purpose.

You've asked better questions.
You've softened where you once pushed.
You've strengthened what truly matters.

This is not an ending.
It's a threshold.

A sacred pause where you choose, with grace and courage,
how you want to live moving forward.

There will still be tired days. That's human.
But now, you know how to return to yourself.
You know how to listen.
You know the way home.

Let this book be your touchstone. Let it remind you:

You are worthy of joy.
You are wired for purpose.
You are the author of your next chapter.

And most of all, you are not alone.

When you're ready, return to the practices.
Reach out for support.

Gather with sisters.
Keep rising.
Keep reflecting.
Keep reclaiming what's always been yours.
Keep rewriting the story your soul came here to tell—
one inspired, sacred step at a time.

Dear Beautiful Reader,

Thank you for walking this path with me.
For turning these pages with an open heart.
For trusting yourself enough to pause, reflect, and begin again.

It's no small thing to choose presence over performance.
To choose becoming over pretending.
To choose yourself, again and again, with courage and perseverance.

I hope these words met you in the exact moment you needed them.
I hope you saw yourself reflected here.
And more than anything, I hope you feel—deep in your bones—that you are not alone.

Know this: you are seen. You are held. You are becoming.
And the story you're living matters.

If something here stirred your soul, let it ripple outward.
Share it with a friend.
With a sister.
With someone who needs a reminder of their own strength and softness.

And as you offer these ripples outward, remember to gather them back to yourself.
Offer yourself the same compassion you so freely give away.

So when doubt whispers, return to these pages.
When the world feels heavy, let your breath guide you home.
When you forget, remember: the wisdom you seek has always lived within you.

Your presence here matters more than you know.
Your becoming lights the way.

With deep gratitude,
Deonne

Keep Blooming

You've done something beautiful here.
You showed up for yourself.
You turned inward.
You remembered truths that may have been buried beneath the noise.

And if you're feeling a quiet nudge that there's more to explore,
here are a few ways we can keep walking together.

- **Follow along on social**—join me on Facebook, LinkedIn and Instagram for inspiration and updates.
- **She Blooms Weekly**—a love note in your inbox with inspiration, practices, and encouragement.
- **Virtual Book Club Circle**—monthly conversations with women who are also on the path.
- **Workshops + Masterclasses**—practical tools for growth, offered online and in-person.
- **Retreats**—sacred spaces to reset, reconnect, and rise (quarterly, in breathtaking locations).

Let this be your gentle next step.
No pressure. Only presence.
The door is open whenever you are ready.

With love and joy,
Deonne

Scan the QR code to explore more
ways to **Keep Blooming**
or visit drdeonne.com/blooming

My Ask of You

If these words has touched you—if it sparked a shift, a pause, or a moment of clarity—I would be so grateful if you helped me spread the light.

Here are a few simple ways you can make a difference:

- **Leave a 5-star review** on Amazon or Goodreads. Your words help other women find this book when they need it most.
- **Share it with someone you love.** A friend, sister, or colleague who could use a reminder that they're not alone.
- **Buy a second copy.** Keep one by your bedside and gift the other to someone stepping into their next chapter.
- **Gather a group.** Use this book as a guide for conversation and reflection—whether in a book club, women's circle, or around your kitchen table.
- **Stay connected.** Join me through my newsletter or on social media so we can continue the conversation and grow together.

Every share, every word, every gesture helps these pages ripple outward, reaching the women who are still searching.

With gratitude and love,
Deonne

Scan the QR code to leave a review on
Amazon
or visit drdeonne.com/review

From My Bookshelf to Yours

These are some of the books that kept me company on my own journey. Each one offered a spark of clarity, courage, or compassion just when I needed it most.

Let them be invitations, not assignments.
Follow your curiosity. Trust what draws you in.
Your next teacher might just be waiting on the page.

The Artist's Way by Julia Cameron
A 12-week creative journey that reconnects you to your inner artist (and child).

Big Magic by Elizabeth Gilbert
A celebration of creativity and the sacred act of showing up for your dreams.

The Body Keeps the Score by Bessel van der Kolk, M.D.
How trauma lives in the body and how healing begins.

Dare to Lead by Brené Brown
Courageous leadership starts within. Lead with heart.

The Four Agreements by Don Miguel Ruiz
Four simple truths that, when practiced, lead to deep personal freedom.

The Gift: 12 Lessons to Save Your Life by Dr. Edith Eva Eger
Wisdom from a Holocaust survivor on choosing freedom, even in darkness.

The Gifts of Imperfection by Brené Brown
An invitation to release perfection and embrace your beautifully messy, authentic self.

The Let Them Theory by Mel Robbins
A freeing approach to relationships and boundaries: let people be who they are.

The Life-Changing Magic of Tidying Up by Marie Kondo
Clear your space, clear your mind, and discover what truly sparks joy.

The Magic by Rhonda Byrne
Gratitude as a transformational force. Simple practices with profound impact.

Mirror Work by Louise Hay
A gentle 21-day practice for learning to love yourself, right where you are.

A Return to Love by Marianne Williamson
A reminder that love is not only the answer. It's who we are at our core.

Signs: The Secret Language of the Universe by Laura Lynne Jackson
How to recognize the loving whispers the universe is always sending your way.

The Surrender Experiment by Michael A. Singer
A true story of letting go, trusting life, and discovering the magic in surrender.

Think Like a Monk by Jay Shetty
Ancient wisdom and practical tools for living with clarity, stillness, and service.

Untamed by Glennon Doyle
A raw, liberating reminder that the voice within you is the one to trust.

The Untethered Soul by Michael A. Singer
A spiritual classic that gently teaches you how to observe your thoughts, release inner blockages, and live in freedom.

The War of Art by Steven Pressfield
Resistance is real. This book helps you push through and do the work your soul came here to do.

Let this be a gentle reminder:
You're not doing this alone. The wisdom of others is here to walk with you, book by book, moment by moment.

Acknowledgments

There are some journeys we must take alone, and yet, we are never truly alone.

To everyone who held space, offered a word, shared a story, or simply believed in me—thank you. You are woven into these pages.

To my children—Alex, Josh, Cody, and Meagan—you are my greatest teachers and deepest joy. I'm tremendously proud of the paths you are carving and the courage with which you walk them. Watching you become who you are meant to be has helped me remember how to become myself. You are, and always will be, my greatest inspiration.

To my parents—Don and Aliene—thank you for showing me what love, resilience, and faith look like in practice. And to my brothers—Derek, Dallas, Devin, and David—thank you for grounding me, teasing me, and reminding me of the roots we share. Family has always been my first classroom.

To those who challenged me—thank you. Growth often arrives disguised as hardship, and you were part of that becoming. Some lessons arrive through love, others through loss, and all are sacred teachers on the path home to ourselves.

To my soul sisters—Rosina, Kimberly, Donna, Kathryn, Sarah, Kaycee, Sheila, Janell, Jo, Elizabeth, Mindy, and Ro—thank you for laughing with me, crying with me, and reminding me who I am when I forget. It is an absolute honor to share this journey with you and witness the light you bring into the world.

To my clients and retreat participants—your courage and transformation have inspired my own. Thank you for trusting me to be by your side as you step into what's next.

To my CHOICE Humanitarian family—thank you for the sacred privilege of serving, leading, and learning together. The dirt roads, village circles, and starry nights shaped my soul in ways I can't quite explain.

To my mentors—Andy, Dave, Jeri, Mimi, Rachel, Ryan, Pat, Melissa, and Teresa—thank you for recognizing my potential before I could see it myself. Your belief in me helped me find my voice, my confidence, and my courage to lead. The lessons I learned from each of you continue to ripple through my work and life in ways you may never know.

To those who have gone before me and continue to light the way for others—Tiffany, Keri, Mary, Nikki, Emily, and others—thank you for your example, generosity, and the fire you keep burning for those who follow. You remind me that leadership is not about standing in the spotlight but about carrying the torch and passing it on.

To my teachers and thought leaders—Brené Brown, Wayne Dyer, Elizabeth Gilbert, Louise Hay, Byron Katie, Diana Krall, Mel Robbins, Steven Pressfield, Jay Shetty, Simon Sinek, Michael A. Singer, Oprah Winfrey, and Marianne Williamson—thank you for showing me what's possible when we live in alignment with our truth. Your wisdom has illuminated my path and reminded me that transformation begins within.

And to me—to the past version who kept going despite the massive amounts of doubt, the present me who continues to rise, learn, and love through it all, and the future me who will light the way back home to my truest self—thank you.

And to the woman holding this book now...
You are the reason I kept going.
You are the reason this book exists.
You are why this story matters.
May these pages reflect your brilliance back to you.

With endless love and gratitude,
Deonne

About the Author

Dr. Deonne Johnson is a transformational coach, speaker, and humanitarian whose work is grounded in soul, strategy, and sacred truth.

With a doctorate in Instructional Design and decades of experience in leadership development, coaching, and global service, she blends practical expertise with spiritual wisdom, inviting women to rewrite their lives with purpose, power, and deep inner knowing.

From her rural Montana roots to leading humanitarian expeditions across the globe, Deonne's life has been shaped by love, loss, reinvention, and rising. She's navigated divorce, single motherhood, health crises, and the unraveling of everything she thought she was supposed to be. And through it all, she's learned to meet change not as a threat, but as a teacher.

She's here to remind you of what you've always known:
You are not behind. You are becoming.

Deonne is the author of *Love from Head to Toe*, a heart-centered blessing book for children and parents, and *From Tired to Inspired*, the first in a growing collection of soul-guided tools and experiences designed to help women reflect, rise, and rewrite their next chapter.

Whether she's leading retreats, coaching clients, or speaking on global stages, Deonne walks beside women in their most sacred seasons of growth. Rooted in grit and grace, her gift is to usher women back to themselves—with gentleness and power. Always reminding them: *the wisdom you're seeking lives within you.*

When she isn't holding space for others, you'll find her barefoot in the sand, reading in a hammock, soaking up sunshine, or dreaming up her next adventure. She believes in the power of authenticity, the beauty of vulnerability, the gift of deep conversations, the mystery of divine timing, and the kind of joy that radiates from the inside out.

Connect with Deonne:
drdeonne.com

From my heart to yours.

Keep blooming.